DUST BUNNIES

DAVE HICKEY'S ONLINE APHORISMS
JUNE 2014 — MARCH 2015

DAVE HICKEY

DUST

BUNNIES

DAVE HICKEY'S ONLINE APHORISMS
JUNE 2014 — MARCH 2015

CONCEIVED AND PRODUCED BY LG WILLIAMS AND PCP PRESS
EDITED BY JULIA FRIEDMAN

EDITIONS DU PIRÀTES

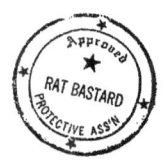

Dust Bunnies
By Dave Hickey

Conceived and Produced by LG Williams and PCP Press
Edited by Julia Friedman

Copyright © 2016 Dave Hickey. All Rights Reserved.

First PCP Printing, First Impression: February 2016
PCP Press
pcppress.com | info@pcppress.com

ISBN: 9781523272662

Printed in The United States of America
1 2 3 4 5 6 7 8 9
Library of Congress Cataloging In Publications Data
2015
Hickey, Dave
Dust Bunnies
208 pgs.

Does not include bibliographical references and
index. 1. Art 2. Art Criticism 3. Contemporary Art

Don't let this get around but Bjork is a Hobbit.

DUST BUNNIES

1. Velazquez had six-foot brushes to do lace and embroidery. This skill faded with fencing fad.

2. This is supposed to be fun.

3. Thin the turkey herd.

4. Don t let this get around, but Bjork is a Hobbit.

5. The Boss is never a fool, however delusional.

6. I have nothing against the students, really. They did what they'd been taught, which they hated.

7. Warhol project: doing it so wrong it's right.

8. Intuition is blink.

9. We tend to die the day before we're born, style-wise.

10. Be York City.

11. Digital slows you down, like serial orgasms.

12. Maybe I should have "participated" more, but I always have things to write.

13. I always find photographs too transparent. There's the whole world. There's a picture of one damn thing, naked to the world.

14. There is a great Walker Evans from the 40's of a sailor walking down the street so briskly you can see the soles of his shoes. R. Crumb picked up on this for "Keep on Truckin'" to place the image in a specific time zone. Evans and Crumb are keen observers. Our walk today is not so spirited.

15. Oh, so Walker Evans is dated? Oh my. I thought he got it right.

16. Painters may be wussy, but one doesn't much like a macho painter. Painting is such a wholesome, prissy thing to do.

17. You don't paint with your dick. Why not shallow, when there is no such thing as depth.

18. When I lecture, people move around, perpetually readjusting themselves. When I show a film, they freeze like statues. I don't like this.

19. I haven't used a projected image for twenty years so my students won't think art is a pink hole in a black wall.

20. DeKooning looks fast. He would paint furiously for about two minutes. Then he would sit in his chair for thirty minutes or so, preparing for the next flurry. Dr J. would do the same thing.

21. Go fast and make a lot of good art.

22. Great rock and roll guitarists just bypass the brain, Ear to hands, quick.

23. Practice, practice, practice. My advice. Not guaranteed.

24. Intuition is how smart people think.

25. I have read Cavell, [we] even had lunch. For some reason, he's hard for me to read.

26. Sometimes your body knows best.

27. Working with ferocity for no particular reason. I don't know what that means, however.

28. Even God, even we, are unaware of our intentions, much less those of an artist. It just can't be done and artists lie when asked.

29. My advice is always: try to fix it. Then paint or build it again fully imagined. Throw the first one away.

30. About mistakes you keep, I quote Julie Andrews: "We'll leave it in, as the Mother Superior said to the Archbishop."

31. Duane Allman used to claim he could see a solo unfolding before he played the notes, but that's genius stuff. Feeling the physical, organizational options, as they proliferate.

32. The street aesthetic of painting has incorporated drawing logic, and drawing logic says you must always be ready to quit and call it done.

33. Language is a prosthetic we all share.

34. Nothing unintentional in this painting.

35. Poetic! Even I am not that old. Pollock is not random. He stacks colors like Velazquez glazes. "Over organized," according to Joan Mitchell.

36. Cloisonné dots are pretty inventive.

37. Cook the dots on cookie trays.

38. Byron was a bore. Fine with me. Wordsworth was boring and not that attractive.

39. My folks were a folk remedy for togetherness.

40. I was influenced by Charles Dickens.

41. High-hearted is the word I use. Ludic!

42. I hate blondes with big boobs too, but there are many exceptions.

43. That's what you're supposed to do with conventional foermats. Go hog wild.

44. You make up the rules.

45. Favorite paintings are like favorite songs. You remember the first time you encountered them.

46. It's interesting that so many women like this painting. They didn't used to. In the 1970's, I regarded Joan and Lynda Benglis as perfectly androgynous artists.

47. Warhol could point out every mistake in every Mondrian at MoMA. He loved them.

48. I like loose painting but it shows up awful in digital. Doesn't seem fair.

49. Wallace Stevens was an insurance executive.

50. Dignity is a privilege of your resume.

51. Picasso, Pollock, Warhol changed to the world. They reordered preferences throughout the world with vast consequences, good and bad.

52. The only thing that won't be denied is undeniable. High bar.

53. Never too late until the big sleep.

54. Been using "haptic, tactile, fractal" for twenty years. Are you catching up, or am I falling behind? These words have meaning.

55. Find a nice young gay gentleman with svelte clothing. Make him into your dealer. The stuff on the shelf is spoiled.

56. Then recruit some critics and find three collectors. You're made.

57. Get on in there with you laig, girl. (Millie Jackson)

58. All three preferable to the flat digital swipe.

59. Another no thought answer pivoting on a pun that makes 20,000.

60. You don't want to know what I'm thinking.

61. Turtles are haptic, tactile, fractal.

62. I think Jerry is sliding off the raft. I don't like hate. I like winning. Inside straight flush on the river.

63. You want me to settle? To find comfort in mediocrity? You want everybody to settle? Than you'd all be famous artists.

64. Somewhere, at some time, you should have paid tuition.

65. I am only fed up with the pervasive notion that the way it is, is the way it will be. Things will change big time for better or worse. When we wrote songs in Nashville: we wrote "songs for the chart today," and "songs for utopia." I always sold my utopia songs with the diminished chords. But it was still a push.

66. I thought stars would shine. Cliques would develop. People would post their ideas.

67. Chuck can paint for sneaky snaps, nothing formal.

68. You can blame painting as performance on Harold Rosenberg.

69. ARTISTS: Live in their mother's basement. Eat pizza. Collect vinyls. Have high hopes in spite fact the fact they do nothing. Wear plaid too late.

70. That is not progress.

71. Not to those who have progressed.

72. Sounds dumb, but I actually looked forward to following your progress.

73. Artists make art. Fact.

74. All of which amounts to self-excused laziness.

75. Who hit the tedium button?

76. Boredom is the mother of progress. Said this before.

77. YOU GUYS ARE ARTISTS BUT YOU HAVE NO VISION.

78. What happens, happens. Children slide off the raft.

79. Dad's doing meth and working two jobs. Mom's puffed up with Botox and smoking Camels. We must transcend this into adulthood.

80. We must be young and knowing and unflappable. Calm and quick.

81. Dublin is square, until you get drunk.

82. To try is to deny one's talent.

83. If you want power, you seduce the powerful. If you don't, have a fucking election.

84. There are lots of ways of thinning the turkey herd. I like deleting because some fool tried, and got rejected. More pain. Less gain.

85. This is not the inquisition. Some contributors just get a little samey.

86. Ru Paul is the best God.

87. Lesson One: The Art World is a rough fucking place where people talk dirty.

88. I have not found it so. Actually, I have not found it.

89. Lesson Two: If you're on social media, you are not making good art or, at least, not enough of it.

90. ART AIN'T A HOBBY.

91. Try this: Ruskin's paragraph implies an envelope of vision. Paintings in which we see more or less clearly than we might, characterize themselves as ideological styles; Pre-Raphaelites, Impressionists, on up to the present.

92. See the show first. Don't waste research.

93. Stones of Venice are great. Fors Clavigera foresees Joyce. Just magnificent.

94. "This is better than that" is not an idea!!! It is THE IDEA!

95. Coloring books are better than digital art.

96. I am bored by dead flat. No magic involved. One little bump would quadruple the information in a digital image.

97. I was working on digital encoding before you were born.

98. No rules? What about very bad habits?

99. I am trying to imagine myself standing in front of a trash pile in a stupid orange jacket. Positioning myself at the end of the tube from a zoom, talking about poetry and spirituality. This is junior level charisma building bullshit with too many props and no detectable raison to be. PBS on the down low.

100. Bob Hughes is to blame for all of this.

101. Everybody has a style. This painting works for me. Notice how the red rectangle is pushed forward and still falls away.

102. Al Held made one good painting: "The Empress of China"—about 1968. What idiot has been telling you about Al Held?

103. Welcome to L.A.

104. Shoot Al and Chuck's paintings on the wall. Tell me which one is better.

105. Late Frank Stellas are not nearly as disgusting as late Al Helds. Most liked is bullshit. One counts by quality.

106. Look at Held with color between the lines. Vaudeville Crap.

107. The trajectory of Al's progress suggests a heartbreaking need for attention—not a bad thing had it not gone so wrong. For me there is just no laughter pr whimsy in Al, which makes me think he protests too much. Chuck is cosmopolitan and witty

to me—like Eve Babitz' act a party. Tres LA. I think He.d was one generation too late.

108. I don't like Held's pouting, but I have also have a vestigial resentment for Al ruining three generations of painters out of Yale.

109. He ruined some painters. I know their names. I think people think nostalgically of Held now because of his clunky innocence. Kids like that. The cigar. The paint splattered pants. He was an abstract expressionist who had no wit and no place to go.

110. The cloak falls open to reveal the mister within.

111. In this utilitarian age its hard to explain that theory doesn't teach you things, it teaches you how to do things a little differently.

112. Ken Price: It's all a gift.

113. I want people to have their knowledge. Mine doesn't work.

114. Many Americans really can't read.

115. Move to Texas.

116. Light that doesn't light anything up.

117. Art is an irrevocably social activity. That why we have to talk.

118. Most new art is an ideological spin on art made forty years ago.

119. I really think art is the future.

120. The utility of French theory is that it teaches us how to speculate, and artists should do this. The utility of Frankfurt School? I dunno.

121. From the start, I thought theory helped me see through habit and fashion, and to see the object and the primary behaviors.

122. Not good word with semiotics suspended between the cup and the lip.

123. Love French. Not much to say about the French.

124. Meaning is reference, even if we're performative zombies.

125. You can't just paint. You're supposed to contribute to a sophisticated discourse.

126. Cup and the lip: Is a sign uttered or heard? Two different models.

127. I prefer objects to pictures. Can't quite tell which is which. Foucault and Deleuze ended up as high pragmatists, I think.

128. Art does not depend on words, at all, ever. People depend on words.

129. Philosophy makes bad art. Good art makes philosophy. You got to let art win sometime.

130. Cultural Theory? Cultural Theory! Who the fuck knows.

131. Flaubert said that.

132. Perfectly sincere, although I have no filters except for mediocracy.

133. *The Raw and the Cooked* is a very good book by Levi-Strauss. Levi-Strauss argues that primitive antimonies like the raw and the cooked evolve into guiding social metaphors in all cultures: pre technological and post. I use the terms exactly as Levi-Strauss used them.

134. I was talking about professor ingratiating themselves to their student by being "cool." The music sounds great. I have no doubt they played about a foot over you students' heads. That's about the right distance.

135. French theory is not only provable, it's self-evident.

136. Excepting Blanchot and Ranciere, who seems to be writing Althusser backwards.

137. My image is exactly what I want it to be. No strings.

138. Frames are okay if there is no painting. Check out early Chuck Arnoldi.

139. Elizabeth Murray's paintings are great, funny and relaxed. She never kept them from doing anything they wanted to do. They are at rest.

140. Jenny's frames are pretty cool. Ashley seems to be in flux. Just like talking to hippies in Austin in the sixties.

141. Painted on frames date back to the eighteenth century. Edit: sixteenth.

142. You can't break the envelope by trying to get into the envelope.

143. I have been a school teacher occasionally, but not recently.

144. I collect drug songs as part of my recovery. "One toke over the line." "China White." "Heroin." "Me and Mrs. Jones," etc.

145. We know Duchamp saw the Stair, but whatever.

146. Only the French could call bd asceticism.

147. Picabia is who Duchamp might have been.

148. The meaning of a sign it the response to it.

149. Most critics do sound and fury. I do sound fury.

150. Painting is just shorthand for, say, a deal with objects.

151. Sculptures are objects you know nothing of, because you have to be there.

152. Critics always want something amazing. Not finding it, they police tropes.

153. Artists are such crumb-balls. Critics are your only friends.

154. Never have befriended an artist. I have supported their work strenuously.

155. Bad artists look at critics with puppy eyes. Not my fucking fault.

156. Tracy Emin looks funny, like she's peeved or something.

157. If you can't distinguish good critic from bad, you very well may have missed something.

158. No critics in art school. They have honor. They cannot survive.

159. I just play by the rules and execute.

160. BEWARD OF THE GOD!

161. Everything forty years old is original.

162. If you have never heard of Mark Richard Babcock Jackson, you are ignorant.

163. This world is totally atomic. There are not enough kindred spirits on the wall to start a poker game.

164. I don't give myself that much credit.

165. Oft heard among my acquaintances: You could help me but you won't.

166. If the "like" button was important, we would all study Wolfgang Puck.

167. The journey starts with a single step.

168. The paths are open before you.

169. "Is blowing." Continuous tenses are more revolutionary.

170. A weather incident. Global warming

171. More a fencer than a fighter.

172. Just wrong, like a lot of other art mavens in San Francisco. Could I look at the wine list? How's the kale?

173. I tend to be dismissive via aperçu. If an aperçu, or an aphorism is true, it is no longer an aperçu or aphorism. At best, my insults are "spun truth."

Consider my insults as bookmarks for my taste. You should know these things.

174. If you think this is "intellectual" you're crazy. This is just me, free associating to help my fingers recover from a malady. I came here to look of clarity and courage—the embers of subterranean society. I still have my mittens on.

175. You're giving Marcel to much credit. He was a hustler. Embrace Picabia. If you need "aesthetics" you're fucked.

176. I prefer the coda to L'Eclisse for evening prayers.

177. After Z point I can never get to sleep.

178. The photographer Lewis Baltz had some Antonioni in him.

179. The director Paul Greengrass of the Bourne movies sweeps a lot of Antonioni tropes across the screen in high-speed swaths.

180. The best thing I like about Antonioni is that he rarely shoots reverses, which lets the camera be where it is.

181. Look up "adagio," find Antonioni.

182. Duchamp was a two trick pony. First he did the urinal thing. We don't need another. Second, he got his collectors to shop with him on 14th street. He would see something. The collector would buy it for him. He would turn it upside down, sign it, and sell it back to the collector for a substantial profit. As good clean fun, I have no problem with this, but in my imagination I see Duchamp playing roulette in Monte Carlo. A squad of German scholars in ski masks, collar him and whisk him off to the German Critic School to

sell a straight-up casino scam to sturdy young Huns. Marcel didn't take himself too seriously, neither do I.

183. If only it took two people to erase it from the canon. Duchamp said art can be boring because at that time Andy was selling boring as a loss-leader, and Andy could be a bore, but he was never boring.

184. Millennials, I have noted, are big on "free." Nothing is free.

185. I would assign two pieces of candy as a reserve price.

186. Foucault would call this disjunctive condition an "An Open Secret."

187. Critique is gathering. Theory is cutting.

188. I imagine about 100 474's lumbering around trying to find the right gate.

189. Fake traditional doesn't work. What about just plain Winslow Homer, not even in video?

190. I like the trash bag menagerie.

191. But does it make a "space for revolution"—whatever in the fuck that might be.

192. I saw an Anish Kapoor show at four museums. I think it was following me.

193. I like Van Gogh's landscapes better than his dorky people.

194. I believe boring people are made and not born. Babies have their moments of coolness.

195. The distinction comes from Auden's *Dyers Hand*. Lord Byron was a bore but never boring. Shaw was never a bore, but he was indeed boring.

196. I dress like one of Waylon's roadies.

197. Like one of those convents where the girls can't chat.

198. That's why I banished group crits in my little graduate program. It works. It frees people up and somehow encourages bonding among female grad students. Dunno how, maybe it puts "daddy" at one remove.

199. Group crits are the site of snotty divisive semi-crits. In the world sure. In a crit where daddy is there to show off for, no good.

200. Solicit feedback from your peers. They are the only ones who matter.

201. Critique turns art in on itself. Theory opens the heart.

202. Biggest problem with group crits: good art is dismissed with encouragement to make more like that. Bad art gets talked about for fucking months to no avail.

203. In school, that was my job. Catcher in the Rye. Often heard remarking in faculty meeting: "Is this a fucking art school or what!!"

204. What students want: a professor who is not an asshole. What students want to be: not an asshole.

205. As a professor I aspired to be an anti-cowboy, dispersing the herd out over the plains.

206. Structuralism proposes that the world is fucked. Post-structuralism thinks it can all be fixed up fine if we don't say wog."""

207. The Future: Dust-bunnies!

208. You babysit and babysit. Then they do something derivative. Then you can help them.

209. Fine in private. Cruel in public. One may be wrong.

210. Hard to imaging sinking lower than UNM.

211. Is Betty Crocker married to Joe Crocker?

212. I do two things in class: I say be free, and I say you're forgiven.

213. I do in class what matters, and you better do that too.

214. Suppression of self-censorship is a double negative. It means what it says.

215. I think things that are there to be said, should be said. Then, if they turn out to be wrong, apologize. This was the principle upon which I wrote a book about "Beauty" many years ago. It was a crazy thing to do but it worked out okay.

216. I have always gotten away with being weak in a strong voice.

217. No group crits for anyone. We want to remove the figure of authority that encourages suck-upism, and unnecessary confessions.

218. I am from Texas. The accident of being born in that evil place has probably cost me five million dollars over the years. I am routinely called a Texan, which

hurts a lot. Women, at least, are spared this insult. Since calling one a Texan labels you as a sexist, racist swine and should.

219. I let you people say things to me I would otherwise not allow, just to see if anything's alive out there. If you meet me don't try it.

220. His reason makes him a very bad writer.

221. Since art is a squadron of disciplines and not a discipline, group crits are more dangerous and destructive than you can imagine. Remember your experience. Multiply by every art graduate student since 1975.

222. My rule for studio visits: If you're not sick, don't call the doctor.

223. In the West of Ireland, "Hickeys" are notorious pharmacists and drug addicts. Inherited that.

224. My faculty question: does the university attract assholes or make people into assholes?

225. Ignore professors: the jewels are among your peers.

226. Art is not anything to teach. Drawing a floating foot from below is something to teach.

227. I acclimate students to the discourse. Tell them who they are ripping off. I can do this because I have actually been in the art world a lot; most of my colleagues had not.

228. You can't make art about anything you learn in school. It's just the raft you push off from.

229. Baldessari and Michael Craig Martin weren't bad.

230. Add up all the hurt and we all have it coming. About self-control, remember Oscar Wilde: We are all measured by the quality of our enemies. Self-control: avoiding dorky enemies. Making enemies is a career decision.

231. Why am I always on the bottom?

232. They keep repossessing my best aperçu.

233. Stay poor, down under the tort line. Talk bad.

234. What is bigotry? I hate figurative panting generally. Am I a bigot?

235. Fact: busy people have no time for mood-swings or fantasies of humiliation. Words and pictures cannot hurt us, and if they do, it's our fault and not the words' and pictures'.

236. Creativity is poison word, use facture.

237. One should probably opt out of war pornography.

238. Oh boy, "real," "depth," "bigotry." Words I don't know that meaning of.

239. Facture precedes academia by about a thousand years.

240. Old black men were there first. Is that sexist?

241. I m becoming more comfortable with collateral damage.

242. The pen is mightier than the sword. If you have a sword.

243. I don't get my panties in a bunch. I have been portrayed as a Texas monkey—we have shorter tails. I don't belong to no fucking identity group. We are here to fight, not knit.

244. Welcome to the media: if it bleeds it leads. It's best to live with crazy right in you face.

245. Expensive propaganda is pens with swords.

246. Americans are scairdy cats.

247. We live in a nation that it 90% racist and sexist. Let's just fucking live with it. As Foucault would say, we want to know where they are and not drive them underground. Let's talk dirty.

248. We're down in the gutter looking up at the stars.

249. We are fighters for fun, not pussies.

250. I try to volunteer flat art only. Digital destroys art, flat art a little less.

251. Do you think I'm just bullshitting? I've already got the money in line, but oh no, it would work. Fuck you all. This is fucking real.

252. Wit, satire, cruelty.

253. I'm looking way beyond white people.

254. Making jokes can change the world.

255. You must read Cormac McCarthy's tragic compliancy.

256. The self-pity starts with *Blood Meridian* and proceeds from there. People in Texas all its Literature. I call it

creme de menthe. Oh boo hoo it's all so sad. Let's have a nice lunch.

257. Fuck the Sixties. Rednecks and Hippies, just like today.

258. More casual sex. I'll say that for the Sixties. Also, Bill Russell transcends history.

259. They were all smack dealers, except for Blue Cheer.

260. This is "Failure Pornography."

261. To these people, painting is anything smaller than a house.

262. Our magazine would have better tits.

263. I am auditioning to be the Thomas Paine of this revolution.

264. Consider the heritage Joe Brainard, Ad Reinhardt, Tom Wesselmann.

265. *Juxtapose* has standards.

266. Obits: a juicy gig! I don't want whimsey. I want cruel cartoons of fat guys waving their auction paddles.

267. New collectors are the same people who pay too much for cocaine.

268. *Coagula*!! A half ass hippy excretion. And how did it change the world?

269. Define humor. That's funny.

270. Humor is funny.

271. The cry of the marginalized sparrow.

272. The secret to humor is pain. We're standing here knee-deep in shit quoting the classics?

273. I like Alex Bag.

274. I planned on forty. Now I have thirty-five years of tarnished time accumulating.

275. Anything after 40 is punishment for having so much fun before then.

276. I'm back in black, and yes, morons like figurative painters, they are always with us.

277. Hard to wrap the Rapture around all the virgins. As if.

278. I've tried every kind of fool there is—settled on Danny Kaye.

279. Only fools took post modernism seriously. It's a wankers' ploy.

280. So you would take us back the Pre-Raphaelites. It's all the artists fault who aren't you, right? "Asses" is a little lumpen-prol for a child of privilege.

281. More Burke than Kant here.

282. I am beginning to suspect that Americans like dystopia. The OJ in Pasadena was a cultural hub.

283. Send them to Santa Fe. All wreckage. They speak to the sublimity of wreckage.

284. I am waiting for it to wash over me like a mighty flood!

285. This stuff just washes away with Glue Gone.

286. This is my only point in my life. Buy my books.

287. A simple "fuck you" will deal with this evangelism.

288. A game without rules, or content gets personal. Just hoping you won't have your feelings hurt by ignorant assholes.

289. The Art Newspaper thinks he's Maurice Lewis! Quoting me. Oh the shame.

290. To those who mention that I sound 20th century. I am.

291. When Andy said I like it, he meant I liken it to something else.

292. I've been a lot of things but never a chart.

293. Larry—too pricey.

294. The bubbles interrogate the cosmic idea of damp.

295. Turrell is the Wendy's of Light and Space art. My late beagle Ralph could understand it.

296. Imminent domain would give me a Pontormo.

297. Check out Gajin Fujita.

298. I would kiss the McCarthy goodbye. Never going to be hotter. Never was that good.

299. Paul MacCarthy—tenured beatnik.

300. Very American. Very Ruthenian. Very gay. Very Pop. Very obstreperous, etc.

301. Filling up my piggy bank.

302. Between simple and complex.

303. Children need objective correlatives.

304. I don't have art buddies. I own art I like.

305. Nothing is better than now. There have been times when people knew what's better a little more quickly.

306. I bought 90% of my art when it was cheap because I believe my eyes.

307. I have subbed out pictures to more insightful souls than I.

308. Sophists? Sophomore word.

309. Sublimation is a senior word.

310. I write so as not to become an old dude cruising the canapé table of late capitalist culture trying to get my friends into "Sleigh Bells."

311. Recorded music and mass murder are the two cruelest gifts of the twentieth century.

312. I mean to see the way we see.

313. That would be Ruskin's innocent eye. I love Ruskin but I don't believe in it. What if I had Campbell's soup for lunch?

314. I know what I am talking about.

315. Except that an athlete "in the zone" is, more properly, completely "in the game." An artist "in the zone" is

somehow dancing beyond it. Degas was often in that zone.

316. Warhol is not really boring to me. Because the running film gradually brings everything into flat focus. The tiniest flutter is a cannon shot.

317. The Golden ratio is harder than it looks!

318. Ruscha claims he was born to watch paint dry.

319. Simone was a brilliant woman but she sort of creeps me out.

320. Being "in the zone" allows you to go slow very fast.

321. I think it's okay to waste a day or two, even a week, on a work of art. After a week, set it aside and finish it in your head.

322. Auden is always to be trusted.

323. Most of my work is extracting ideas from the oral culture.

324. I believe in walking thru museums fast until something stops me. Then I slow down without boredom. Lotta crap in the world.

325. This brings up the main problem of art history classes . You have to look at slides of a lot of bad art. A là *Clockwork Orange*.

326. Whenever you walk through a museum, especially when you're young, you are going to find yourself liking a lot of the wrong things. Never ignore this. You might be right. The future may be nestling in that improbable piece of goo. Or you may be an idiot. These are good things to know.

327. I can't remember being young and stupid.

328. Millennial gets to heaven, asks Saint Peter: "Will there be snacks?"

329. The Ramones at 78 kick ass.

330. I used to take speed to stay up for three days. Then I could slow down into a real good nap.

331. Do you prefer the pasture or the sidewalk?

332. We only know we're going slow if we can go fast.

333. Slow ride: Foghat.

334. Friction fast burns away the skin. Friction slow is sex.

335. One rule: If it don't fit, don't force it; if it's too tight don't fight it, if it feels right...well you know.

336. The lick is "Sweet Home Alabama" is very nice slow. I know this because I learned how to play it. Slow was the first step.

337. Especially since no one knows what "depth" means.

338. You tell me reading is hard. Isn't that what we were suppose to do, we Masters of the Universe?

339. You want to win and you can't comprehend prose?

340. If art was easy, you would be doing it to broad acclaim.

341. Difficult novels are useful. Poetry leads one into exegesis.

342. Infinite Jest is a rewarding slog. Unlike the web you can't hurry.

343. Unlike artists, monkeys never make the same mistake twice.

344. I keep expecting a large mouthed bass to break the surface.

345. Piketty's *Capital* is okay, kind of Simon Schama's MA Pop.

346. This problem: an anti-authoritarian idiom achieves power and authority and becomes a fascist poem.

347. With lists. Power points. And xeroxed essays by Hal Foster.

348. I think my point is that when it comes to theory, I am not a profesorre but a humble school teacher.

349. How can I put it? We don't even know the shapes of the theories we teach.

350. You don't go all in on "untrustworthy."

351. Empiricism in art. If it's not there, it's not there.

352. We are probably living one in our slipshod way.

353. Eden can be debated. Utopia not so much.

354. Foucault turns the middle crazy. Maybe he's right.

355. Eden has every thing we want.

356. I would rather talk about doodle-bugs than architects.

357. I remember McLuhan. Catholic dude.

358. Shoppers want. Seminarians need. Self-mastery seems redundant.

359. Ignorance can read something wrong at exactly the moment it turns right.

360. I am a serious Francophone. I just don't like them, you know.

361. Theory is a playground. Approach it as such. If it hurts, don't do it.

362. We all know that.

363. All this linear comes from someone else's book. You run over something with a tractor it's obsolete. There are 360 directions that future might take on a flat plane. A million would be easy.

364. Good and bad rate straightforwardly. I am only arguing that good design, as defined, is bad art.

365. It simply means that good design occupies a neutral position—a "fit". Good art moves off that position.

366. Style is a word much fraught.

367. Some misfits are failures. Some are Veronese's forced perspective.

368. Good design is the absence of bad design.

369. Dave is telling you that "The Forever Now" is not forever.

370. But the new Mona Lisa is different from all the old Mona Lisas.

371. It's very interesting to me to regard bad art as false prophecies.

372. Full disclosure: I probably like Alexander because everybody hates him.

373. Dunno about qualms. I've heard people have them. I've been looking a Michelangelo too, A little twee, but there's some promise There.

374. Jerry Saltz is mini-me.

375. Fuck you, he said mildly.

376. Best way to be informed is not to read evil texts.

377. Ordered a "quattro venti soy latte" the other day. Four fucking languages to order coffee in Santa Fe."

378. When their toes aren't blue, Chicagoans live in perfect denial of the cold.

379. I once took a cab one block in Chicago. The driver was an ex-art-grad-student. I tipped him.

380. I keep forgetting you people don't do books or the liberal arts. My bad.

381. Arthur was not a good writer or thinker, although a lovely man. I remember standing with Arthur and his wife in front of Miro's "Battle of the Insects." Arthur remarked, "Now who's this by?" I told him because I'm evil.

382. I don't take anything seriously enough to write a blog about it. That's almost as corny as a Ted Talk.

383. Thou art spared.

384. Zizek is writing all that stuff I decided not to on account of its' being corny.

385. Paul Schimmel can do that.

386. I write all the time. Sometimes I write on social media. Mostly I write shit [people] can't understand.

387. Just today I got a real clear factual view of the educational accomplishments of the art writing community. Now I'm wondering why I signed up on this ship of fools.

388. I'm trying to give what you like. No hard words.

389. Routledge is a Chernobyl.

390. The point is you seem to want a video game that is professionally difficult, where you play a professional pool player, play poker with a real poker player. I am a real fucking writer, exasperated at the moment with junior Varsity. Get some chops. There is no crying in art.

391. I live on the edge of autism.

392. Or what if I am a woman! I heard on TV the other day that smoking fucks with your Y chromosome. In any case, if I have smoked myself into womanhood, I'm still a lesbian.

393. In my experience, you have to sneak up on the future, or you end up sounding like KISS.

394. I think we strive for subversive sociability.

395. Video is up there with "Bob Dylan" and "Futuristic" and it started off so great!

396. I think it's getting more local. If the ocean is not up to your front steps, you go out for pizza.

397. The compensatory option is easily handled by having more anonymous sex.

398. Art that compensates for you being a dork.

399. A bullshit show—I saw it—hated it.

400. The post-human world begins when it turns out we can't breathe methane.

401. Standing on the same fucking pedestal.

402. High school rules I would like to change: Faux naif is actually faux. Art therapy actually works. The future will look futuristic. Twenty-year-olds are a great source of political wisdom. Surrealism is sincere and not a horrible mistake.

403. Surrealism is defunct at Chez Dave. It's just painting pictures.

404. For philosophy I prefer Charlie Watts.

405. Another note: I was able to detect the source work for every one of these works within two seconds. A cruel person would say this is art, if custom cars are art.

406. I worshipped George Barris but in a different church.

407. Stop it because "precious" is not a major league skill.

408. Art with spiritual explanations ain't safe. What the fuck is "spiritual"?

409. Major League in my book is what you don't have to be told.

410. Joyous and Amazing: Major league.

411. I disagree with nearly every major critic, except we all like Matisse.

412. Back in the seventies we did our own acoustiguide about a Whitney Annual, about how somebody got it with a blow job, or an ounce of cocaine or anything sordid. Sold like hot cakes.

413. Gide quote is very nice about Vuillard. There's a great one at the McNay in San Antonio.

414. You know the rules so you will know what you're doing when you break one. Are you breaking good or breaking bad? Morse Peckham says is all about breaking rules. I tend to agree, if they're breaking good. Mostly what I see today is "slob art." Prayers unanswered.

415. They would be non-cosmopolitan, suburban artists from Lansing, or somewhere like that.

416. My solace is that some students listen well and I see their questions in their art.

417. Many academic rules are wrong.

418. Veronese can do that sometimes. Not many others.

419. Titian painted the white highlight squiggles when his atelier had finished the painting. Students cannot be trusted with white.

420. About bad color: Imagine any painting or sculpture. Now imagine it as if the color was right. I rest my case.

421. Drawing is very 17th century. Drawing divides. Color unites. Pick 'em. Richter says all abstract painting is a parable of social relations.

422. "Should" is a very big word. You don't have them all. You have a toy piano. What about magenta off to taupe? Of course we can imagine colors and shape, imagining is about images. If they are any good we name them: My favorite "orphanage green" Ronnie Landfield could do that.

423. Bauhaus is the ebola of art.

424. It's never a good idea to presume that stupid is good, although sometimes is is—barring literacy.

425. These are colors turned into linguistic antimonies. Color is a field not an equation.

426. That's not magic. That's because two colors juxtaposed are different colors.

427. No magic, just cones and numbers.

428. Trout is a cool color, although the Dutch nailed it. Some colors are colors, others are similitudes like trout and coral.

429. Color blindness is a prime cause of dyslexia.

430. Dyslexia is almost never about language. Also "Sno-Cone Green" is my favorite Benjamin Moore color.

431. Dislexia is hell for those I know who suffer from it. Siri can't understand my accent. That sounds like a market wedge.

432. Maybe my computers wrong. More yellow in vermillion. Fuck Siri!

433. Ronnie Milsap, the singer, had perfect pitch. He could sing numbers into the telephone.

434. Color is the soft promise of immortality: put bunches of roses all over my coffin; they deaden the smell as they bear me along.

435. Ellsworth can see color: We were walking out behind his studio. There was a local pine branching out over pale green grass. Ellsworth could see the atmosphere of purple generated between the two different greens. He pointed it out to me. It was there. I felt so ashamed.

436. Albers was an asshole, but Goethe was an idiot. I would have thrown the book away except it cam from the library.

437. Gray American. Grey Brit.

438. Grey sound greyer. Lucky to have my last book published in London. Grey motherfucker.

439. You do realize that our self-deprecation is why we're not Jerry Saltz?

440. Cheating with white is a studio axiom.

441. Emotion is caused by thought, so around we go.

442. I know that you don't have to be nice to be good, but I suspect that there is an entire continent of color that

is overlooked in Albers's synopticon. South America, I think.

443. The room I am sitting in is painted taupe.

444. A wall of taupe will sustain small paintings better that Arctic White or anything thing else. (BM 1358).

445. This may explain why taupes are so receptive to colorful paintings. I've used that particular BM taupe a lot in exhibitions. My taupe is dark and way down on the blue.

446. About names of colors. I can read music. I have pretty good pitch—I never fall back on names or numbers or writing it out except in a formal crises. The same applies to color. I suspect.

447. Rauschenberg hated Albers.

448. Bob didn't much like "professionals."

449. Bob was a savant. He thought he knew all that shit, maybe he did.

450. Bob's real name was Milton Rauschenberg. He changed it to Bob, so all the "Robert Rauschenberg" shit is academic posturing.

451. You don't want to know the color-blind art critics. There are quite a few.

452. Someday, I might go through this and count your excuses for being ignorant. Children see more color. No they don't.

453. Any book will do in the absence of good ones. You just [have to] to the update yourself.

454. The internet is not a library. A shelf of library books offers a gaudy bouquet of collateral knowledge and information. The book right next to it. The book above. The book with the red cover you never heard of—like that. The internet doesn't do spontaneous tangential little gift.

455. The plague of specialization seems to have set in. I don't play the oboe, but I like the noise. Open your hearts.

456. If you're old you're happy to be alive. What's to be sad about? There's a lot of life in two or three seconds.

457. If Hank Williams sucks, how bad is everything else?

458. Using the quickest, most accurate word doesn't make you a snob.

459. There are no free lunches but there are some cheap lunches in the narrative of civilization. Ankor What!

460. My point, I guess, is that the sisterhood of the arts is real, and all about frequencies.

461. I think some of my friends are rather overlooking the threat precognitive sensory translation poses to all contemporary critique. Makes me think I was right all along.

462. Real Life is: People Fuck Power.

463. Oscar Wilde: We'll be down in the gutter looking up at the stars. No stars on social media.

464. There are artists beyond ridicule.

465. My point. My point. This is jejune.

466. Language is a prosthetic.

467. So Derrida might say. The prosthetic reference is his.

468. Wimps to the left. Wimps to the right.

469. Drove my cart onto the beach, which I shouldn't have done, but it was so great: jungle, beach, waves, breeze—black out. Woke up seven hours later in the hospital having been found about 150 yards into the jungle. They told me I shouldn't have been driving on the beach, but I knew that. That's why I was doing it. Lovely scene to die on, but I woke up with dirt in my eyes covered with bugs. One doesn't recover from a penchant for recklessness.

470. What the fuck is a lush photograph? A selfie at AA?

471. If art takes a lot of trouble, we should take lot of trouble.

472. Are the Waverley novels reverse engineered?

473. Like *Ivanhoe* and *Rob Roy*. This is the past, just like I pictured it. Science fiction and historical fiction are the same genre to me.

474. I read all those sci-fi books as a kid because they weren't set in Texas.

475. My meta problem is that we have somehow dispensed with history without dispensing with its cultural directionality. It can all go wonky.

476. Problem with growing up, we start making looks-like things that look like us.

477. Problem with technological breakthroughs like custom steel: just because you can do it now, doesn't mean you should.

478. Form is function, which is part of the problem.

479. None of the sic-fi bashing means that "Snowpiercer" is not a pretty cool flick.

480. The art world runs on ennui, which rather presupposes that something new might happen from time to time.

481. I want a stamp that says "Futuristic" to stamp on bad works of art.

482. The Lucas building is horrific, like an amputated tit. More "Dune" than "Star Wars."

483. An Unidentified Female Outrage.

484. All it needs is heart plugs.

485. Better a cataclysmic metaphor.

486. Which intellectual? Just interested. Met a professor the other day. He said he was in "Theory." I asked him, "Well, what's your theory?" Silence was his response. Maybe he writes better than I do.

487. Don't move to Portland. Too much rain, intensified by too many fountains.

488. I am expecting weak defenses and sorry excuses.

489. To be perfectly honest, any books will to if there are many of them.

490. Defense of no education. Distrust of reading. Is this the Tea Party?

491. Any book, even a bad book, is better than no book.

492. I shoot'em all and let God sort 'em out.

493. There are no dogmas, just rocks skipping across the river.

494. More wisdom than knowledge.

495. Sanctimony is holiness on stage. Sincerity is candor on stage. Cynicism is skepticism on stage. All are self-serving theatrical tropes.

496. One may avoid these malaprops by writing about something.

497. A rancher friend of mine, when told that he had a romantic profession: Ranching is blood and mucus up to the knees, Ma'am.

498. The blood in the henhouse renders one insensitive.

499. I would vote for Cape May as the epitome of human folly.

500. Do not mistake anything on social media for writing.

501. I prepared myself for a lot of shit jobs when I set out to be a writer. I tried to limit my jobs to work rather than labor. You just do it to get what you want to be.

502. Like if you're a real art critic you ignore artists. They are totally tangential.

503. I consider artists a nuisance too, with certain exceptions. They think I should agree with them. I always tell them that if I want a burger, I don't feel obligated to be friends with the cow.

504. I like some art by dead artists. Don't you? Or is it all about "community"?

505. Which product do you prefer: the burger or the bullshit?

506. Carnivores dine together. Herbivores dine alone.

507. There are no longer any full time artists. And it shows.

508. As a critic, you want to be the first or the last.

509. Rhetorical questions are always rhetorical, but there is more to rhetoric.

510. Yes "critical discourses" is a cliché. I meant bundles of words with weird words sprinkled throughout. Such bundles, I fear, may be empirically isolated.

511. I am a recovering Celt.

512. My grandfather was excommunicated by the Church in Galway and Tralee for revolutionary activity.

513. Thomas Paine: bass player for the revolution, holding it together in the groove.

514. Irving is as treasure.

515. All they want is jokes and straight lines so they can make lame jokes.

516.   I love the little prefect museums.

517.   Forty years of sucking can be exploited, as the Neo Expressionists were, but usually to no good purpose without an aesthetic re-do.

518.   Forty years of not quite sucking, like Mark Tobey, is more plunderable.

519.   Those beyond ridicule.

520.   Winners and losers [are] born, not made.

521.   I think I agree with David Hume that culture is that which survives its maker and its patron.

522.   Fine dining for me are those artists whom we have forgotten are good. Fairfield Porter, Hassel Smith, Neil Jenney, Alfred Jensen.

523.   The gardeners at Brown threw away two major Anthony Caros. It happens.

524.   You know it when you've failed it.

525.   We all became what we are to get laid.

526.   If you admitted that you all do the same art, you could make adjustments to suppress redundancy.

527.   Vegas would be Chicken-suit Central. Actually, the chicken suit is irrelevant. The sense of cultural permission was very special for me, just the lightness of the evening.

528.   Every good work of art brings with it an aura of bad shadows.

529.   New is different? Rule of Ennui?

530. The difference between the secular art world and the academic art world is that in the secular art world you can still be friends with idiots. Academia as a cauldron of hate. We forgive, up to a point.

531. I had a job moderating a panel at Cranbrook. They refused to pay me, claiming that I was an immoderate moderator. No brag. Just fact.

532. Idiots, in my vernacular, are beyond ridicule.

533. If you don't think you can change things, you can't. Stop.

534. A Biennial des Refuses.

535. Okay! I think we're ready for sting-theory.

536. Bookies in Vegas, the line-makers, the princes of the point-spread, are very brazen.

537. I long for better equipped quips.

538. Irony is ruining our culture. Sarcasm is almost necessary.

539. I'm not trying to be smart. I am smart. That's different.

540. I'm sorry if I seem snarky. It's always been a burden.

541. I'm sorry if I seem patronizing. It's always been a burden.

542. Cards in play. Always apologize. Never explain.

543. I expect more from everything and often get it. Not [every] time, of course.

544. Play AM radio in your garage. This will discourage nearly all critters. A lot of people say pissing in your garage will discourage raccoons I told my wife about this but she didn't want to do it.

545. The University of California Press is assholes. They print a masterpiece and won't reprint it, not even in paperback. Academic Philistines. I'm so sorry but I think I'll keep both my copies unless the press comes around to collect them.

546. I will twist in the air and fly up my own ass.

547. The Philistines, like figurative paintings, are always with us.

548. I have chunks of barbarians in my stool!

549. All I need is a doorman. It's either democracy or it's not. I can't imagine the fun I would have missed if I had been more discreet about women.

550. Your doorman, your telephone, and your drummer should always be black.

551. Life lessons from another barbarian? Have we demoted John McCain? What about Bill O'Reilly?

552. I can recognize a twofer when I see one.

553. Until I discover that civilization, I'm staying home with milk and cookies.

554. I am a condescending hypocrite. Is that something I should work on?

555. I stay out of Texas. My life depends on it.

556. I am a statue of limitations.

557. My brain is getting reports by telegraph from my emotions.

558. I do a take or step or two down the road to public availability because I am in it for the "difficulty." If I explain something difficult, it might help the paperboy. Actually, I am an advocate of intense exposure. When I had my gallery in Texas, the mailman and the paper-boy, who came in everyday, acquired a very good sense of what was going on. They developed bullshit detectors and even took pleasure in things from time to time. They reveled in just knowing things. I could see them opening up like little flowers.

559. That's what art critics do. For the moment. I'm watching skinks.

560. Schadenfreude: crepuscular happiness or satisfaction. Your mother in law is driving over the cliff in your new XKE.

561. I approve of your staying close to the world we live in: skinks and XKEs—the road to redemption.

562. More whine for my men!

563. Bad people who can't afford to be.

564. You think this is all no charge. You better hope your name and your art never crosses my desk. I exact revenge almost carelessly.

565. I don't [do] objective. I do justice!

566. Social media is like Vegas. It's such a far-flung vicious metropolis that I look at it and think it is about to offer up something profound. It doesn't. Vegas doesn't either, but it's more fun.

567.   I was the only gentile in a B'nai Brith Scout troop. For a while, I was the only straight guy in Soho. Gronk thrives on otherness.

568.   My fellow scouts wrote these long poems about all the shit gifts they got for their Bar Mitzphahs. "Thank you uncle Herky for the not too perky ring/ Damn you Uncle Herky cause you turned my finger green." Like that.

569.   Rap schmooze!

570.   A lot of rap is in hexameters, beginning with the *Aeneid.*

571.   To be "in the zone" is to be one with the game. Art is not a game.

572.   A sophisticate! He's playing a game. One shouldn't.

573.   I don't think entertainment is invading art's territory, rather the reverse. Richard Prince, he said, Richard Prince.

574.   Facile is what social media understands.

575.   I have no problem with digital except that it is an antique medium for cutting edge art. You got to go someplace fresh.

576.   I am holding out for "critical dust bunnies."

577.   We did a new genre every four years from 1850 until 1970.

578.   Artists would have a say in the way the world changes if they weren't so pathetic and provincial.

579.   (Dave leans back in his chair, wrist to forehead.)

580. I don't know many Formalist, Texas white guys. I just think that visual art should be, in some aspect, visible.

581. Reify is a good word to describe Richard Pryor.

582. Modern? Creativity? These words mean?

583. I didn't mean you were apes. I think you have been educated by apes.

584. If you're going to be profound, be more funny.

585. I think the apes should speak French. It would so much more "civilized."

586. Just like TV commercials, "production values" have gone up.

587. Tech is not where art lives. Art does the opposite, unless you are anxious to gurgle in the mainstream and get on TMZ.

588. So that's where we are. Bruce Nauman and William Wegman are boring? Great.

589. Ignorance is bliss. We don't know everything but we should know sort of basic doo doo.

590. 1972 was fucking great!

591. Who the fuck cares about "images"? Are all of you guys in Hollywood? They do "images."

592. So you don't like fetishization? Why?

593. Bruce did the triangular plywood room with yellow light. But he's Bruce.

594. Commercials on TV are better than the shows. I like the Nissan "Peaceable Kingdom."

595. Video art mostly exists on "Video Day" at your local museum. They have coffee and sit in the dark, which is pretty much what they do all week.

596. Two things I hate to do standing up: Read and watch TV. Sex standing up requires more commitment.

597. Twenty years ago I walked into the studio of a video artist at Art Center. There she was: the only artist I ever met who had the sense to customize the TV set to match the palette of the video onscreen. I thought it was great! I have never seen this again, although someone out there must have stumbled upon it. Duh. Duh. Duh. Live in the world!

598. "Clown Torture" and "Instructed Mime" may be my favorite videos. "Instructed Mime" is sublime, he said, sounding like a Cockney.

599. That would destroy Venice. A sign posted in the sand: No Clowns!

600. The one-year-old inbred redneck is the problem. Not the computer.

601. That's also why we can't paint like Raphael. Proprietary secrets.

602. The death of history doesn't seem to have changed the stochastic flow of...like...time.

603. If you guys are thinking about "sincerity" and "intimacy," keep it to yourselves.

604. I nearly sneezed on a sand painting up by Four Corners. Scared the hell out of me.

605. I am beginning to suspect we grew up in a golden age, although it looks like bottled piss from here.

606. Say this to yourself as a mantra: Digital is SO over. Digital is SO over, etc. until tea time.

607. Little sticks and naked Barbies will swamp digital.

608. In many primitive language yellow and green are not distinguished.

609. Artists have not always embraced technology: That's why we have impressionism and all of its consequences.

610. The Mayan solution: let it all fall down.

611. All the time and work I wasted learning how to make a living as an unpopular writer. Now you're telling me I should have been begging my congressman all along. Honestly never occurred to me. I always assumed we invented the future by trying to make our way. Cha-ching.

612. [NEA] did a great deal of harm. It subjected young artists to the taste of older artists creating positive censorship. The NEA told its panelists they couldn't know the names or sources of the slides we watched. They also told us to privilege women, gays, lesbians, and people of color. One couldn't know "what" the artist was unless the art was "about" what the artist was: i.e. "Identity Art." This was a bureaucratic catastrophe that still echoes in the halls of academe.

613. Sleep in your car. I did.

614. In NYC, one may sleep on the subway, in the big beautiful public library or in all-night cinemas. I did. You can go to the Cloisters for a little vacation.

615. Plato was a smart guy—though a Nazi.

616. Rigor is a developmental concept. It must change. We must recognize its new standards.

617. Real problem with patronage. European culture is hierarchal. Founding Fathers didn't like Hierarchy. American culture is adversarial. Nobody is ever going to agree on anything.

618. Public funding for art is like "educating" the public to "like" art. Oh Please. This is terrible and ignorant place and art is going to elevate the serfs? Gimmie a book to read and go home.

619. Thing about art. You can always get it back if you stop learning.

620. Seattle was tons of public art—all bad.

621. You want a Saturnalia, slaves in the role of masters? Move to Vegas.

622. Europe is the two-bit cesspool of privilege. You people are genuinely on the third rail. How can you say stuff like public funding, public support, public education. The public can't ever read.

623. With it's varying levels of economic sophistication, I think you have to be careful to distinguish commerce from capitalism in the United States.

624. All of this to replicate the German Kunsthalles that privileged culture over art, to show blue blocks of ice melting into a tin pan in a storefront in Madison,

Wisconsin. You had a space, no money to ship, no money to insure, no money for security. So you showed blue ice.

625. I had sort of professional art world friends. Critics are Kleenex. Artists blow snot into them and toss them away.

626. I liked Agnes with her rosy cheeks, but I did not track her. Also, it's hard to have schoolmarms steal home base.

627. It's a long way from the Cockettes to Bob Gober.

628. The years of the AIDS epidemic were genuinely horrible years. In my little practice, all the critics who should be writing the things I am writing now died scarred and crazy. The AIDS epidemic really was a government-sanctioned plague. This is a republic of shits.

629. I visited an artist's studio in Santa Monica. The kid looked like an Auschwitz survivor. We talked about flowers and shrubs. Two days later he was dead. You just couldn't hold your head up.

630. I should be smoking cigarettes in my little room, but no! This ain't Key Largo.

631. PTSD for every child.

632. My favorite Stones' song. We played "Torn and Frayed" and 'Norwegian Wood" using those weird "Whipping Post," triplets.

633. Universities? Populist? Egalitarian? Oh, I believe that.

634. Nobody tells me anything.

635. Oral sex is usually okay.

636. Unless you're a Platonist, bad writing can't have good ideas.

637. Andy and Serra were all that remained.

638. The consequences of that evacuation are still echoing through the contemporary art world. Nothing was ever redeemed.

639. Lucy Lippard's Daddy was on the board of Yale or something. There's got to be an excuse for all that lame prose. The law that frees us today is tyranny tomorrow. Just because you're free to do something doesn't mean you should.

640. All the women I knew in the art world were pretty much in control of their bodies. They didn't need a dean to keep them safe.

641. You make you own in crowd by not hanging out with losers. Max and I did some good business together. Tuttle is a blue chip artist. I think Louise was genuinely awful.

642. I kept chasing the egrets around the common in my golf cart. They would do like one flap to evade me, but they wouldn't fly. Finally the King of the Egrets looked over at me. He said, "Okay, Dave, you're such a fucking aesthete!" They all took off at once. It was really lovely.

643. I can't doc and drive.

644. Lots of women artists leading a renaissance of gestural painting, but nothing yet that would make me put my hand in my pocket.

645. I think the artists at the slip constitute a rather influential center point.

646. Want to know the heart's distance between Rauschenberg and Judd, Captiva and Marfa? Fecundity and emptiness. I like both. Fecundity makes for a more attractive personality.

647. I am in what they call the Curator House. I can tell that a lot of icky people have been here.

648. Back up there: Werner is great but he's not a Venezualan.

649. Anything in Florida that you wish sanitized, you must over-sanitize, then you go back in a week and do it again.

650. Purple Kool-Aid, plus egrets and sea grapes. I just chased an egret around the common in my golf cart. I wanted it to take off, but it wouldn't.

651. I've been checking out the skinks.

652. No surf—surf in Daytona—over on the Atlantic Coast. The Gulf just lies there contemplating itself. The Gulf and the Atlantic make Florida weird. The water always seems to be on the wrong side of wherever you are.

653. A deficit of skinks on the Gold Coast. Great flowers.

654. I used to live in Ocean Beach. Dog Beach was there. Heaven for Ralph the Beagle. He would chase the waves back into the ocean. They would attack again and he would scamper back. Ralph could do this for an hour at least, like Cuchalain, the Irish superhero. We had some skinks and a squadron of renegade parrots who dwelt in the palm outside my window.

655. All three Ralphs have perished. Don't get old. Your dogs die

656. He hated baseball. That was a joke I got from Andy's brother.

657. I wanted to talk about the projected drawings but there weren't any in the show. I think Andy would have loved to draw like Tiepolo. He was such an aesthete.

658. "Designers" never quite crop Andy's drawing to the page. Mumble, Mumble.

659. Andy loved the republic.

660. Andy painted gorgeous paintings, and obviously he was a formalist. Most of Andy's critics are "purely conceptual." They also think Andy was ironic and he never was, just very shrewd.

661. The idea that tea-and-crumpets Alfred Barr validated New York as an art center is stunningly whimsical.

662. I was right from jump. Open up your eyes. DeK[ooning] and Andy defined American color.

663. Also, this in passing. The original hostility to Andy in the art world was more sexist than homophobic. There were lots of straight-acting gays guys in the art world, but even Bob and Jasper were turned off by his being an effeminate queen.

664. Well, rigor still exists as a virtue in painting, lotus eaters not withstanding.

665. Robert Ryman? He's rigorous.

666.   There is really a lot to hate about Andy, but it was hard to do. He was so steely-eyed and staunch in his convictions.

667.   I hate depth. I have never encountered it. I hate creative. Just doesn't exist. Invention does.

668.   Creative presumes creating something that didn't exist before, an organism. Art can't do that. Today, it's a corporate term. Depth, being depth, is so absolutely imperceptible that I can't really believe it's there. People usually mean repression when they say deep—it's a social-code for the inarticulate auteur. I can't imagine applied "depth."

669.   What is shallowness? Do you live in Berlin? I am confused by this whole oceanic vocabulary. I am, by the way, not trying to be contentious. I just feel a small obligation to be consistent about magical thinking.

670.   I am very tentative about revealed religion. [It] confirms Peckham's idea of creativity as a bastardized, commercialized form of grace.

671.   But you "know it when you see it?"—A Renaissance definition of things invested with Grace.

672.   I may "know it when I see it" in the sense that I may want to look at it more carefully. My eye is innocent, I hope.

673.   I think Andy wished for an Americanized version of ancien régime painting. This is similarly true of Jack Wesley.

674.   Andy's lateral business model has had some influence in corporate culture. About art, suits don't know shit.

675.   Best fear the piper. Also, have you guys ever had a blancmange? Y'all are like that sometimes. Oh we hate business. Oh, we love Lexus Liberalism. We want an office with a parking space to await the rapture.

676.   I should point out that my problem on social media is my problem with poker. I only play offense. Sorry.

677.   I feel like I'm trapped on Weird Al's website.

678.   Why would one write/say "coven of old farts"? Because of the 'V' s. The line reads phonetically: Ku Venah Vold Farts More euphonious.

679.   You have two 'k's, okay? Vs and Ks are at the heart of Belles-lettres writing. Suppressing them also makes nice smooth academic line.

680.   Micheal has recast the work of art as a withholding Jewish father whom you worship while he never notices you. We are about 180 degrees in disagreement. Even so, Michael is sensitive enough to have seen the distinction.

681.   Asked about imitators, DeK[ooning] said only he could do the bad ones.

682.   This note: Only DeK[ooning] could do the bad ones because all of his imitators knew how the picture was going to turn out. Bill didn't.

683.   Artists are plagued by a lack of conversational topics.

684.   I fucking live for my "readers."

685. If your guitar player plays shitty, you can tell him to practice. If your young painter paints shitty, he will tell you he is going for that "shitty painting" look.

686. One further note: The reason you can't paint a DeKooning is that you are chinchy with paint.

687. I don't think anyone paints from the gut. Better for me to say that DeKooning painted passages from Frans Hals much enlarged. I don't quite know what "from the gut" means.

688. Size matters.

689. The academy is down there in DeKooning. Also, I don't think the erasure was a novelty. Soon after his erasure Rauschenberg's work was awash with DeKooning.

690. I am not talking subject. I never do. I'm talking five square inches of Hals rendered in heroic scale.

691. Interesting to me: a lot of women artists are wisely ripping off DeKooning these days. He is a place to go in this moment.

692. There are lots of "little spaces" in DeKooning's paintings. They are almost subliminal.

693. A true artist means there's only one, or a secret society. Also, if you don't think DeKooning is still in the culture and there to be learned from, watch TV. Look at a basketball shoe.

694. Francis Bacon is a commercial illustrator and a drama queen.

695. I can look slow very fast.

696. Lucian Freud is a commercial artist and a drama queen. The UK is about theatre in the same way the US is about music.

697. Mystics are seated in the loge.

698. Cynic is just the flip side of sentimental. Oh! All my hopes are dashed! (wrist to forehead)

699. DeKooning painted faster when there were figures and shorter marks.

700. Pollock may paint jazz. DeKooning paints Dutch.

701. Stravinski: Anyone who doesn't draw on tradition is a forger.

702. A forger only paints what he's copying. I think that's Igor's point. I think that's Libby's point too about assemblage.

703. Bacon and Freud are an acquired taste for Americans because of all the drama. Commercial art? Who's better than Andy? Illustration? Norman Rockwell was great. Decorative? Who's better than Pollock? Feminine? Oh sweet Jesus, that's the dark ages.

704. I love those "lipstick" DeKoonings from the seventies.

705. The Picasso painting film is pretty revealing.

706. All I've noticed is that the little flurries begin a little smaller than the scale of the gestures in the painting and then get bigger. This is just an informed Impression. A lot of "painting out" in DeKooning.

707. Pretty nice stuff about Picasso's choreography of marks as the fill up they rectangle.

708. Glenn Gould's Goldberg Variations are really thought in motion.

709. Intention is bullshit fantasy. We have the work in extension.

710. You get drunk to get drunk. Booze is easy to score and easy to use.

711. Andy thought everything was chemistry. I do too. Get off "bad habits," you wee Puritans.

712. Dennis Hopper, Grace Slick and I did a panel. Dennis claimed that you could fill up the auditorium with the coke we'd done.

713. The black and white Richters in Saint Louis are super.

714. Clyfford Still ain't. I was looking at one at MoMA and a piece of paint fell off. Eeek! The damn thing knew I hated it.

715. Richter is Alec Guinness.

716. Glenn Gould and Duane Allman are sort of titans.

717. Brice? Outsider Art for New Yorkers.

718. We are way off in the suburbs here. Where did we go wrong?

719. And Guido Reni was a pathetic gambler. Thus the proliferation of St. Stephens. Thank you, dice.

720. And don't even whisper Christopher Marlowe.

721. Many feminists have noted that artistic hysteria is the product of womb-envy. These guys actually think they're "creating something," and have a right to be hysterical assholes.

722. I look like I'm carrying one these days.

723. Most freshmen in art have only heard about Van Gogh's ear. They find this appealing.

724. I only rely on clinical information to calm the hormones down.

725. Joan took no prisoners, and couldn't tolerate friends.

726. We shouldn't talk about Ab-Ex without talking about Bradley Walker Tomlin, a very good artist, despised for being a homo. The good old days.

727. Schjeldahl told me this. He was at party in the Hamptons. DeK[ooning] lived next door. There was a knock on the front door. The host opened it on a girl with a torn dress, a black eye and scrapes on her cheek. The host asked her if she wanted to go to the hospital. No. She wondered if the host had another bottle of whiskey. The good old days.

728. Well, when we lived in caves, relationships were more...uh...concise.

729. The gay hegemony in art and culture in America was the result of two drafts for two world wars. Most folks agree. Better that than eugenics.

730. Dr. J used to think the whole game out in his head before it started.

731.   Julius Irving, the virtual inventor of modern professional basketball.

732.   Early Cindy Sherman is the farthest thing from duplicity.

733.   It not what you have. It's what they think you have.

734.   The artist's truth is bullshit. Read Vasari.

735.   You hear a lot about the "artist's truth" here in Santa Fe, a town without any.

736.   I used to love corny Robert-Motherwell-type titles like "Vulcan in Agony." I also love the title drawing from Ed Ruscha's book of found-phrase drawings: Guacamole Airlines (or "Wacky Moliere Lines.")

737.   The opposite of lying may be compliance. "Don't let the bed bugs."

738.   Sincerity is theatrical honesty, usually a making device.

739.   Poker is about reading people. Art Criticism is about reading manifest non-verbal behavior in paintings and sculpture and various trash bins. All such "art" has its own claim to autonomy. If you think your art is about you, then you must plan on immortality so you will always be around to testify on its behalf.

740.   Our detecting of masking or duplicity in an artwork is less often a fault than a signifier of "difficulty" for which all have a covert longing.

741.   Great liars make bad readers. I was just passing on a card player axiom. Here is why I think it might be true. Great Idiots presume sincerity. Great Liars

presume deception. This means that neither have a baseline for truth. This means they just don't know. Equally dangerous predispositions.

742. Artists, as a class, are not that "aware." Most of them aren't even awake.

743. I would rather see a painting derivative of somebody good, than your "original" creepiness.

744. Art not quite severed from the artist's ego.

745. Post-painterly Abstraction refined Ab Ex. Nobody refined Pop but Cindy Sherman. Jeff Koons drops the last little turds of Pop.

746. Replace them with bad photos off thin pieces of wood leaning against the wall, but do not replace McCrackens.

747. Most of the practitioners I knew thought they are re-invigorating pre-modern genres in painting. Portraiture, History Painting, Genre Painting, Still-Life, Landscape, and the Odalisque.

748. Ruscha owes a debt to surrealism.

749. Ground rule: don't get good too soon. You'll spend your fucking life with your high-school sweetheart.

750. Reasonable. I don't write for artists. They have limited vocabularies. Eeek! Dish!

751. I live in New Mexico. One big thrift shop.

752. If artists constitute an "identity group," if they all agree on basic tenets, we only need one artist.

753. I am the servile assistant.

754. Timbre, pitch, melisma, dead spaces, bad grammar.

755. Those are the noises we make being verbal.

756. Non-verbal is really yours. Language, as Derrida remarked, is prosthetic.

757. Showing in prose is tedious. Always, tell!

758. Always tell. First law of prose. When I was in graduate school they used to say "show don't tell" but it doesn't translate into written texts.

759. The dew was glistening on the grass the morning that Pete and Alec went out to have sex in the weeds beyond the brook! Oh please.

760. We do need to know what we're doing. And I'm not teaching anyone anything.

761. That is the moment as it is, and not in your imagination. Don't be a Philistine.

762. Learn not to do it. Learn what your friends really think.

763. I have a Bullshit-Detector 6. Got my first one from Hemingway, who invented the term.

764. Okay, no more poker, ever. Even so, I feel there are good readers and bad. I am above average. Interesting point: Good liars make bad readers. I still watch cable news without the sound just to watch John McCain's blink flutter, a pretty reliable tell, as is no blinks at all.

765. That's how I play. I never confront really good players; I prune the marks. It's like sweeping the

leaves off the sidewalk. In passing, face is better than body. You can teach your body.

766. Trust no one. It's always about the money.

767. Banksy? Is that a boutique bank?

768. Art parties are business. Never drink. It makes you nice and gets you fucked over.

769. There used to be this TV show called "Lie to Me." All about this shit.

770. Is fun for me. Art slows life down. Criticism slows art down. They both help.

771. So much depends on fabulous shoes, especially at Larry G's parties.

772. Skid marks on My Heart.

773. Cocaine dissolves your autonomy and makes you think you're smart. It does help talking idiots. Makes everything so, so interesting.

774. I could make about seven minutes if the girls were semi-naked.

775. My favorite boring obsessive thing, usually on account of meth, was copying the phone book in very neat printing. Also, " Lie to Me" was cool: Tim Roth played such a seedy little asshole.

776. Tom T. and I were once arrested in Wichita, Kansas, because of our imperfect grasp of Kansas liquor laws. A contemplative dude.

777. Roger, Townes, and I were born at approximately the same time at All Saints Hospital in Fort Worth. I

used to say that as long and Roger and Townes were around, my indiscretions would remain unnoticed. Ooops!

778. Who was it died saying "More light!"?

779. Dying is easy. Comedy is hard.

780. Check out Jack Kerouac's recorded meditation on the Three Stooges .

781. You learn the language of non-verbal expression. Poker is very fierce.

782. You gamble every time you cross the street.

783. Math and stat provide the portals to all social speculation.

784. Problem with being a "reader"—you learn things you don't want to know about: fear, aggression and deception.

785. It's always there, if one can read. Math and stat are not disciplines, they are in the hard-drive. You just kick the leaves away.

786. Once, bless us, I drew a royal in diamonds with a king/ten down. I actually won some money too because the filling two holes is so improbable.

787. I should note here, also, that probability is doo doo in poker. You play the players.

788. I play quiet and goofy.

789. Mark Bradford's allusion to Leibniz was correct in my opinion. We don't know we're counting, but we are. Music is ecstatic counting. So is sex.

790. Agnes did not look. She painted.

791. When Agnes was in a hospice, a collector friend of mine asked her if he could open the blinds. She said: Please don't.

792. Daunting to me though. My last words will be "Goodbye Ellsworth. Goodbye sky. Goodbye cookies. Goodbye puppies. Also, trees."

793. There is also the option of not turning into an asshole.

794. How many Deadheads does it take to change a light bulb? You don't change it. You want till is goes out and follow it around the world. This from my friend Butch.

795. Never stepped through that door flung wide before me.

796. Reasonable assumption: Jerry bought Apple stock.

797. Not many real artists around.

798. I said Lou was a great artist. I never said he was nice. He learned cheap from Andy.

799. Everybody reads minds. I just read faster.

800. Profound inner arrogance and nice go together. Rauschenberg, Ruscha, Chamberlain, etc.

801. I am growing tired of "artists' bitching about money. Envy is a scuzzball vice, especially if you envy people for getting things that you don't want.

802. One of my worst art world moments: I was in New York having drinks with women of a certain age,

which would be my age. I mentioned that I had just tossed an invitation to Jeff Koons' birthday party. One of the ladies broke down in tears. I could have given it to her! She could have gone to the party! Sheesh!

803. About Louis Reed: I never thought of him as a prophet, but as a gifted, wry companion on the road through it.

804. I went along on the Rock and Roll Animal Tour. Eeeek!

805. I do remember Whitey Glan, the RRA drummer, remarking that you could drive a D-Train up Lou's butt. Probably an exaggeration.

806. My favorite line: The dust that Pancho bit down south, ended up on Lefty's mouth. Just too good.

807. Luis [Jiminez] was one of my first artists in my gallery in Austin. He ran off with my gallery girl, but that was what one did back then.

808. Hillbilly Shakespeare.

809. Luis went around with a lot of deans. He also got pissed when people at his black-tie museum openings tried to order drinks from him.

810. All I learned in Texas was how to hate.

811. California has waves.

812. Billy lost his in a sawmill misadventure. He claimed it helped sell songs.

813. My life has been like riding an inner tube in New Braunfels.

814. Just don't try to vote, speak out loud, or get an abortion.

815. Jerry Jeff Walker is from Manhattan and it shows. When he moved to Texas, I moved to New York. There used to be this bar in Manhattan with an iguana cn top/ All the professional Texans hung out there. This was good because, at least, I knew where those fuckers were.

816. Pee Wee came from heaven.

817. Every time I ride up the Taconic, I'm looking for the Headless Horseman.

818. When I told the lady at the airport I was going to South Bend, she said, "Well, get a haircut and get a job."

819. What can I say? My mother was frightened by the OED.

820. I like words that sound good. I love the word "veranda."

821. That's why I studied linguistics, to learn my medium.

822. It is not about communication. We do not communicate. We correlate. Nothing gets from my head to thine undamaged.

823. Theory does propositions. Academic Critique does connections. A lot of academic critique is about theory, but very little is theoretical

824. Getting out in front is not theory. It's prophecy.

825. Good theory, from my perspective, Barthes, Foucault, Deleuze, puts its foot in your face.

826. Post Minimalism is nearly as toxic as Post Impressionism.

827. I don't know any modest professors. Even the good ones are closet narcissists.

828. That sounds fair, accepting the fact that one usually writes for the "phonotext," the soundless sound of writing in your brain. That song. The difference between reason and rationalization is too close to call.

829. If we all could sing like Al Green, nobody would do anything else. Civilization would collapse into ecstasy.

830. My practice exists where art meets music. Not where art meets suburban liberalism. It's fault, but it's empirical.

831. Why should writing be simple? Life's not. Also, the thing I've liked best is teaching. The worst places I've ever been are universities.

832. I honestly never think about artists unless they're seated beside me at dinner. Then I try to keep their hands out of my plate. Gronk hates "needy."

833. Cookies!

834. Andy would steal the fox stole out of your closet.

835. Critics are just plain criminals who leach off your God-given talent. Uh Huh.

836.   Empirical theory can accommodate dissonance. Rational critique has a harder time with this.

837.   I asked Meyer Shapiro a question at an opening back in the day. He told me to take his classes. From that point on I avoided poseur professors and relied on The Two Leos: Steinberg and Castelli.

838.   I am distrustful of any art that might fit within the etiology of surrealism.

839.   Start a foundation and pay yourself a great deal of money.

840.   Meyer Shapiro. I was directing gallery in Soho when he snarked me off. I felt dissed and amazed he thought I was too young to talk to. At that time I could have bought him a house.

841.   I am going down to Captiva. I will check on how Rauschenberg's foundation is designed. Artists do this all the time. It gives them access to public and private funding. All you have to do is give a pittance here and there to some jam drummers.

842.   Street is street. Cred is cred.

843.   Don't know, but elephants have shorter memories than I do.

844.   I prefer Mapplethorpe in the category of muscular lovelies.

845.   The art market ain't much to complain about in a racist state. Also, yes, I am not invited anymore. Also, yes, I will die pretty soon. Also yes, my literary expectations in the media have been reduced to the possibility of good spelling. Also, despite social media, I remain I "lumber-jack" writer. If I write, I

feel a tree must die. My problem today is that most of the artists and critics I know are so individuated and so fierce, that it is impossible for me to imagine either group as a "constituency" or an "identity group." They are just random crazy people out in the drift.

846. My heroine.

847. If you're tenured, you live forever.

848. Nobody needs any help, nor does anyone get any.

849. Snooze-burgers in this jaded virgin's view.

850. My connected friends are so connected they think survival requires a condo in Brussels.

851. My only good DeKooning quote: "I make pictures about a crazy world. They say I'm crazy."

852. "Too many" was not in DeKooning's vocabulary.

853. I went to a party at Elaine DeKooning's loft, which was above Herbert Ferber's studio. There were enormous crashes and clangs from below. We all looked concerned. La DeKooning said, "Oh, that's just Herb snoring."

854. If you guys are dedicated to zombie abstraction, could you please make it better?

855. The past sucked. The present sucks differently.

856. But how sad we would be if it didn't suck, and we were responsible for our own disasters. That would destroy me.

857. I think we should be calm in our little rooms and dream of the innocent, untainted future.

858. Meds were invented to screw around with.

859. Shallow is not bad. It's just not German.

860. Sincerity is for sissies! Fashion is all there is.

861. Couture exists because many women have modest breasts.

862. I love Jack Wesley. His high heart can lift you up.

863. Sincerity is theatrical honesty.

864. Candor is sincerity with cojones.

865. Style "Craft", "Chops," "Sincerity," "Content," etc. None of these terms mean anything in particular, but you need to have an answer ready if someone slips one over the net at you. Something glib to close down the conversation.

866. Sincerity always presumes an available audience. That's why there is no such thing a "sincere" writing, although Phillip Lopate tries.

867. There isn't any if the artist has successfully stitched him or herself out of the work.

868. Strong understanding doesn't help much if you lose.

869. All of your enemies perish, singly and in groups.

870. You can see farther if you stand on your enemies. Ideas are like streetcars, one [comes] along every few minutes.

871. I am a happy subaltern.

872. I do not write criticism for artists.

873. I get mental tinnitus after about an hour of social media. Chatter, Chatter. Chatter. Mostly me chattering.

874. As we say in rock and roll: Shoot the wounded and save yourself.

875. I am the arbiter of freelance practice, being the last one working.

876. You can be a prima donna at the museum. Never, never, in a gallery.

877. Always write the story they want, not the one you want. It's all just writing, in any case.

878. Talking about writing freelance.

879. I feel the same way about drinking.

880. When pressed for funds I go the Chunky Soup route. Too snobbish for Ramen noodles.

881. I mostly just want a nap by any means.

882. I am on it like a duck on a junebug.

883. Worst part: you got to get there early to park. Then you can't leave.

884. That's because they write sad things and know not what they write.

885. Throwing one's money away is fine. The people who worry about you throwing your money away are not to be trusted.

886. .Grace Hartigan was an okay painter but not a nice lady.

887. William Faulkner: One 'Ode on a Grecian Urn' is worth any number of little old ladies. I haven't decided yet, although I have acted ruthlessly in pursuit of my interests.

888. I would agree with that. Winners are winners from jump, even if they lose.

889. I admire good parents. I know about six.

890. If you have a kid or a job, the best working time is from 3 to 9 in the morning so you can get up and work before anyone reminds you that you are a slave. My life for decades. You got to do it.

891. Cost of doing business.

892. 4.5 hours max sleep for me forever. Probably ruined my life.

893. Just remember: You can sleep in your car but you can't drive your house.

894. Gypsy invitation in a motel restroom in Santa Rosa. "Call Darlene. Good sex, then death." I think Terry Allen found this one.

895. What I write today means I will have Wheaties in eight weeks. What I wrote eight weeks ago, buys my Wheaties today. It never ends. Deadline. Deadline. Deadline. Death.

896. High standards. You may live in Slobbovia.

897. Curran can't paint. Does paint as if with baby shit.

898. Craft. No mistakes. Mistakes are everything.

899. Who, I ask, would think about craft?

900. I think of craft as "Can you draw a horse?"

901. Good craft creates what I call the "crisis of technique." If I, as a writer, learn how to make you cry when I want you to. Can I do it again with the same maneuvers without undermining the integrity of my work? No, I would say. This is to say good craft, once achieved, must move toward entropy. Otherwise, it's masturbation.

902. Craft is like shooting jump shots. Great jump shooters have forgotten how they do it. Great craftsmen have forgotten craft. It is body-knowledge. You thinking about craft, you ain't thinking.

903. Masturbating in a museum might be fun. Watching someone else do it is not.

904. If you have reduced it to body reflex and know when not to do it. The point is to seduce the rules, not abide by them.

905. If it's good, I always want to buy it. Sometimes I do.

906. If we spent a little less time planning and more time improvising on what we have planned, it would be more fun.

907. To get in the door you need a little talent and a little craft. The doorman takes it all away from you and you start again against the big people.

908. Craft is a trap. You can master it and still not be any good.

909. Rules are important. Only one life, remember?

910. Great! Now get a haircut and get a job, as they say in Lubbock.

911. *Working Space*—good book, kinda sincere A-. Buy it.

912. Always too much Bono. I stayed in his hotel in Dublin. That was okay.

913. I read "Information Theory and Music." That set my clock ticking.

914. Aristotle: Possibility is comedy. Probability is tragedy. What we want to happen is funny. What we expect to happen is very sad.

915. These objects have markets outside the object and the art world. You can chip'em off, like officers of the Raj, and send the home to Leeds.

916. Art supposedly has value as its unitary self.

917. Markets for gems and art are both scarcity markets. Gem prices are not vulnerable to aesthetic whims.

918. We all must send special thanks to the Judd Children and Kienholz' wife. I was talking to Larry Johnson on the phone: I told him Kienholz died. Larry hoped this wouldn't interfere with his production.

919.   We're all a little slow today: Diamonds and gold have their own markets a million miles from art. Since the Renaissance they have been treated as intrinsic costs in artist contracts. That world. My simple point, when Marxists, who hate talent as much a CEO's, started insisting that artist should be paid first for their labor, they stopped being paid for their labor.

920.   When the parts are worth more than the whole, the widget itself is problematic. Also show me a good collector who hasn't been stung by the viper of Situationism—they show with Barbara Gladstone. Also, Marxists and snobs are all the same in Kim Philby Land. It's the lower-middle-class piece-workers (artists) everyone hates for their jumped up vulgar little dreams and ambitions.

921.   I am in the value business.

922.   One-of-a-kinds have no retail platform.

923.   Please let it be known that I spent my MacArthur subsidy learning to play Texas Hold 'Em in Vegas Casinos. This was a wise vocational decision.

924.   Baby talk only works with dogs.

925.   British Press makes the Mafia look like Sunday School.

926.   My best love song was called "Police Girls."

927.   Police girls got the keenest apartments/ where they don't keep planters and they don't keep pets/ Police Girls when they leave the department/ like TV dinners and cigarettes.

928. I used to write songs with my ex Martha Marshall Chapman. It could get bloody but it was always fun. We also invented tackle-Scrabble where you put the dictionary across the room and had to fight to get there. I loved to lose at this game.

929. Here is what age will do to you. Up the page I fully intended to type "nude tackle Scrabble." but my poor body has been so beat up and racked by Nude Tackle Scrabble and other diversions that I couldn't bring myself to. So now I am feeling less than candid. So: Nude Tackle Scrabble Live with it.

930. A lot of you are coming out for love as opposed to romance. In my view, love is just too...uh...eternal. Romance dies so there is always that elegant death wish, that urgency to get it all in quick. I love the panic of romance. The certainty that it cannot get better. The part where you lift up your feet and you don't fall down.

931. We start from romance, love, or something like it. It's one step to music, one step to poetry, a million miles to Chelsea. Murmur, murmur.

932. Quick is better than deep on social media, and in life, too.

933. I suspect criticality, like representation, is local fashion for dividing things up, into pairings of "this" and "not this." Always bearing priorities.

934. Presumed criticality invariably "doubles" things. Andy is a genius. Andy is a whore. You pick 'um.

935. Jeff, in my view is too slow. I'm bored with them before he finishes them. His works leave dinosaur footprints.

936. I would opt for kinesthetic over telepathic. Telepathic is too sci-fi. Also, I really don't care about makers.

937. Presuming that there is always a sub-text is not good critical practice.

938. Way back up there: My favorite Darwinian critic is Morse Peckham.

939. It's usually not new but it's different in the moment.

940. There are always issues of precedent.

941. Young artists are always looking back to find that moment right before everything started sucking, so they can push off from there.

942. What if it's bad art? The whole proposition presumes that the art in question is pretty good.

943. Not sucking is a very personal decision. My rule of thumb is that we hate our fathers but we love our grandfathers because they always gave us a quarter.

944. I suspect that our whole idea of art changes every forty years or so.

945. Forty years is a market cycle, don't ask me why.

946. We are in a Fabian, Paul Anka moment, music wise.

947. I think masturbating under a shelter in your exhibition is really really dead.

948. Christopher Knight calls this "The New Competence."

949. In Grandfatherly influence the ideology changes but the "look" is appropriated.

950. My granny was very wise. She told me that "fair" happens once a year and usually in the country.

951. I'm still waiting for the cynosure of dust-bunnies. I'm not seeing change, I'm feeling boredom.

952. We're certainly diving for the mainstream in this moment.

953. Now that the Dean of Fine Arts has a vote, I think it's more random than we could ever imagine.

954. Meaning is reference. Foucault. We cannot live without it.

955. Lubbock is equidistant from everywhere.

956. "Kind," E.M. Forster said, "Then kind, and finally, kind."

957. I saw Wayne County hit Handsome Dick Manitoba over the head with a mike stand. EEEEK!

958. Autumnal Riley. Rigorous Agnes. Ungiving Truitt. All like that. World-class artist. My contemporary!

959. Agnes was a bit daffy.

960. I am never daffy but I can generate commensurate chaos.

961. Agnes was eccentric and had a right to be. Agnes was no kind of crazy, she was a chop choo train.

962. I do art. I say whatever I think about it, even if the blessed virgin painted it.

963. I saw some Max Coles and Anne Truitts today. I just floated that out. Just stop it with 1974.

964. Comparisons do not suck. They are the foundation of criticism.

965. Swirls before pine.

966. I know too much art; Actually my preference for Cole may have been influenced by two Truitt drawings in the room. The ones with the white paper face and the colored paper just barely extending beneath the top sheet. Nice drawings, but took me of an Anne Truitt tangent.

967. The quarrel builds the discourse. It never ends.

968. What do I do? Mention Max Cole and get fifty comments reminding me she's a woman. Or mention Max Cole, the women, and get fifty comments snarking me off for the admission.

969. I was sitting in a room with two Max Coles and three Anne Truitts. On this occasion, I liked the Coles. This isn't the Dean's office. Sheeesh.

970. First pot-luck dinner is SoHo marked the end. Had to take a cab down from Fiftieth to eat Dean & Deluca amidst toddlers. Eeek!

971. Not much for peer-wrestling with children present.

972. Jackson Pollock is folk art: Check out the window on the Pacific Shore Lounge in Ocean beach. Sign says: No shirt, No shoes. No problem. Mondrian is a big folk-offender: That means they won.

973. Abstract Expressionism was not an idea—it was a tradition of large pictures that owes its size to the

scale of Mexican muratisté painting and to the gestural tradition of western painting that began with Titian. The paintings were big and wonderful but they were no biggie. Freud and Marx were brought into the discourse to make them "important"—to give them an historical and psychological ambience that signified European solemnity. For myself, I have always found the paintings ludic—if a little too noisy. Painting are just paintings. Talk is just talk.

974. Pollock painted to Dixieland, made bebop. Great feet. Great wrist.

975. "Liking things" in Warholese also applied to showing how things are alike: The soup can and the Rothko, the piss-canvases and Pollock, Marilyn, the icon and the image, etc.

976. Soup was slang for ab-ex surfaces. Andy put the outside on the inside and vice versa. My source for this is nothing more than factory chatter, but it's plausible.

977. I hold with Don Barthelme who didn't want things to "look funny on the page."

978. Can't you just add exotic words like "taco" to the dictionary?

979. Jesus, priestly protocols. I just want to type, not experience the rapture.

980. Ovid didn't put spaces between the words either.

981. As taught: poison: Teaches us to be brief and simple. Many problems to not respond to that agenda. Global warming comes to mind. Chaos theory helps. Not brief, not simple.

982. Andover is not a school, it is the gateway to privilege. Ask Frank Stella.

983. When I was in sixth grade in Santa Monica, a counselor who had trouble with my chronic truancy told me I was one of the ten smartest people in L.A., Bullshit, of course, but, from then on, he let me come and go as I pleased. That makes me weird.

984. Heartless but correct.

985. Trying not to be Eurocentric. A friend asked that question. Huey P. Newton, I think.

986. Driving across the Mississippi into East St. Louis. Drummer in the back seat wakes up and looks out the window. "Gee," Rowdy said, "this is all bunged up!"

987. A safe story: One white guy (me). One black guy (Rowdy). One symbolic bridge over a symbolic river. One urban catastrophe. Perfect.

988. Actually there is a weird curve on smart and stupid artists. Art gets good when it hits the wall. Stupid artists hit it faster. Smart artists have to think their way through to the wall. Takes longer.

989. Poor and bright scares people.

990. The economic privilege that makes you nice is not much good in a very long dog fight.

991. Nordic people are über-strange.

992. I am just tiptoeing to the door. Can't write about white people. Only swinish elitists do that. Can't write about black, brown, Asian, or gay people

either, poaching on profs' turf. White guys can't do that. They just don't understand anything! So fuck me. I'll kick some Nordic butt.

993. Paintings are social objects.

994. Richter says abstract paintings are allegories of social relations. That's too German for me. Makes Mondrian a racist. I do love Richter's "painting out," of course.

995. I especially find the black and white blurs very cataclysmic.

996. That horror is symptomatic of provincial painting in the USA.

997. The world is empty and without redemption out here in the boonies, so I am going to fill it up with gewgaws and whimsey.

998. About Richter: Gronk say nothing before the Baader-Meinhof paintings is any good.

999. I always thought, if the MoMA was indeed a museum of Modern Art, Jim Brooks and Norman Bluhm should have a retrospective. Norman made some bravura paintings. Instead we get an actress in a glass box. Be still my heart.

1000. We don't understand the news cycle or box-office. Tilda in that box.

1001. I call it The Great Dumb Down. Irwin, poor man, is still killing painting, even though his work only relates to painting these days.

1002. Funny is the handmaiden of despair, but I am very funny.

1003. You guys are such good Americans: Morality trumps Quality because morality is mostly about not doing things.

1004. Resistance to the swoony invitation is easy enough if you have seen people die. Good old Camus, forever young.

1005. I get skateboarding on the freeway dreams. I know what they mean.

1006. Anti-Texan is always welcome.

1007. The art business is like the newspaper business. Every day we run around trying to fill the white space that confronts us.

1008. Museums do pay artists fees. They just don't pay you.

1009. I've never received adequate compensation, but I never expected it. There aren't many of us dancing on the edge of the wing.

1010. A glut on the market of artists also depresses prices. Art-worker! Are you a creature from the past?

1011. Themes are one of my night beasts.

1012. Okay fine. Disregard good art. Let the dogs out. The MacArthur Foundation called me a "genius." I ain't nor do I know any. Every time I find a real genius she dies.

1013. Harold Bloom, I fear, may have gotten one thing right, by dating the birth of the avant-garde to the birth of theatrical self-consciousness in Hamlet.

May not be right, actually, but it seems like a cool fulcrum.

1014. Disney s *The Mouse Detective*—the world of Richard Tuttle.

1015. I live to "improve" the art world.

1016. Installation, since you can't buy it, or take it home, leads to 20-second art. This is usually more than enough. The practice has degraded into mixing influences. Plywood rooms, things on a shelf, piles of aggregate matter, and patio furniture (or Paddy O'Furniture, if you will). Bob Gober and Bruce Nauman are always exempted from anything bad, however. I once saw a warehouse full of dildos in brown boxes. That was conceptual.

1017. The old days sucked but the art has lasted better. If you like slave labor, you will long for the good old days. Every generation of artists thinks up their own solutions.

1018. If you are from the Galapagos, live in Vegas, and don't like M**r**s*y, you can be on my team. My theory of Chattenegro Noogie is that it arises from bad racism and a good sense of euphony, and childhood memories of "Glenn Miller and "Chattenooga Choo Choo." Mixed blessings everywhere.

1019. I don't have any work or any future around art. A little bit daunting, but natural enough for seniors.

1020. My grandfather got excommunicated in Tralee for "revolutionary politics."

1021. I do love the theater of argument. Maybe more Edmund Burke. He writes good.

1022. My quadruple great grandfather was Jonathan Edwards. A drama queen of the first order. I keep trying to clean up the mess he made.

1023. My political strategist has advised me not to snap back.

1024. One might say of Bloom as a wag said of Ruskin. "He has the English language on the tip of his tongue. Would that he had some in his head!"

1025. Protecting the innocent is what you do if you're not.

1026. Reasoning and rationalization are too close to call.

1027. Steroids, johns and women's body building in Santa Monica. Sunshine Noir.

1028. Movies unhinge me. I rewrite them in my head. I also perk up the palate in remembered cubist paintings. I also cut out all the streets between Canal and 48th in my dreams of Manhattan.

1029. Nothing is clear but it's technicolor.

1030. Nothing is very far away in Ireland, with the exception of Grace and Forgiveness.

1031. And, as they say: Would ya be catholic?

1032. Devolution is not a joke.

1033. Bowles is word for word is a very fine writer of prose.

1034. Camus cares. Bowles does not.

1035. Bowles' novels in my view are powerful narratives in which Bowles doesn't like his characters. This lack of affect can be disturbing to Care Bears out there.

1036. I knew one phrase in Mandarin from the early seventies: Can I have more straw for my mattress—now forgotten and unnecessary.

1037. For ten years in New York, I knew one professor, and he was a jerk.

1038. I have lost jobs over women's rights, have you?

1039. I liked Leo. He called me David with this weird German-Italian accent. He mentored me and treated me like the paper boy. He was interested in women, art and money, in that order. We were not friends, nor did I wish to be, but he told me great things.

1040. Most of you could and might be my grandchild. Sorry I can't give you a quarter.

1041. In L.A. we spelled Fluxus with an "F"—what a mighty tide of wonderful art.

1042. I am prone to exasperation in the hometown of feckless exasperation.

1043. I usually use girl names because ideological artists are fierce, but not well acquainted with the discourse. I have book coming out called "25 Women"— about the work of women artists, so the kid walks the walk, okay.

1044. I ran a gallery in Texas where Latinos were thick of the ground. Luis Jiminez and Mel Casas were two of the first artists in my gallery—even though the latinocrats hated them for reasons we could never figure out. I have seen Celia Munoz' work over the years and she does have beef, but it's more aesthetic and racial. The problem I confronted width my Latino students here in New Mexico was that they couldn't leave town. They were totally imbricated in the local culture. I had a student whom I could have sent to Yale or Harvard, but no matter how famous he might have become, he still had to show up every Friday and do the books at his Dad's store, and it was a very nice store, so money wasn't the issue, Family was.

1045. I am like one of those Junior League charity ladies who want to teach the tango to black children. Feckless but sincerish.

1046. "Glue-gun art" was a bad word in nineties.

1047. Peers will win every time, if you choose good peers.

1048. I am really getting sick of artists having to support their own support systems. This is a work of weenies!

1049. When ARTSPACE asked me to consider art for Father's Day, I nearly lost my lunch.

1050. When I was learning to write, I would always stop for time to time to read a section of "Tender is the Night," to remind myself of how high the bar was set.

1051. Have you been reading Adorno again? For him it's false-this and false-that. Snore-burgers.

1052. I saw "Deep Throat" in a theater three times. Linda never made it to the Whitney. An artist in an unrespected medium.

1053. There is a difference between being an elitist and a separatist. Separatists can drink Jamba Juice and talk about the old school Orange Julius.

1054. Mike Kelley built a good relationship with Christopher Knight. I think Chris wrote three positive reviews. All subsequent criticism just pilfered Christopher's words. Two-man game.

1055. The blonde leading the blonde.

1056. My rule: Don't let life ruin your day.

1057. I love the ephemeral smartypants people. Why would that be? Who was the funny downtown woman who said she liked democracy because communism was too boring and fascism was too exciting?

1058. I am not Henry Miller. He liked dwarves and I have never developed that particular kink. I still like Velazquez, however.

1059. Interesting: Kenneth Burke credits language first and foremost with the invention of the negative, and as a consequence, the invention of tenses (the not-now) and of complex continuous tenses like the future imperfect: "By tomorrow, we will have been running, etc." Scott Fitzgerald is the master of these nuanced tenses, but no Thai double negative? Ouch. Maybe that's why I had so much fun at the Tiger Den, the first place I ever say a white guy with a bandolier of ammo.

1060. Had a class with the grumpy KB when he visited UT. Eeek.

1061. Or I was rather young. I misquoted him somewhere and he sneered at me for two months. I was abject.

1062. So we have Neely and Greeley—beginning to sound like the Grand Ole Opry.

1063. I was standing on the bank, leaned over, and toppled into the mainstream. Forgive me. I'm really into dogs and drugs.

1064. The last work of art I encountered that came without an excuse was Tom Stoppard's "The Real Thing." Walked out of the theatre feeling pretty light.

1065. It's always my fault, so I've been told. Couldn't be that I am dealing children from the Village of the Damned?

1066. It's all a long way back but I have no trouble conjuring up Titian banging in those finishing touché of zinc white, measuring out the Golden Mean.

1067. Canada fucking rules!

1068. Medici and Borgias wanted bling, not bullshit.

1069. The ecstasy of Canadian Flamenco!

1070. Here's what happened. "Zinc white" is more euphonious "Zine-quite." "Lead white" has no bounce. I always go for euphony over facts, but I really was wrong. Still "zine-quite?"

1071. Optimism, I would suggest, has nothing to do with tomorrow. It quantifies the élan with which we face the moment.

1072. All the art critics I know work for major corporations. I have a low tolerance for suits, and they for me.

1073. It's hard to rhyme "social practice," but you are the professional.

1074. Caravaggio: "I put the beautiful angel's butt in the middle of Flight into Egypt to articulate my homo-erotic social practice. I am just so angry, you know?"

1075. Since we die and people can't read, it is very dangerous to make art that demands the living presence of an explanatory auteur.

1076. We don't demand intellectual curiosity and empathy from anyone in the art world. So rednecks are going to be curious and empathetic is the face of professional apathy? If this happens, I will fly around the garden.

1077. I did not resign from art. I fly to New York when I can, stay in a mid-town convention hotel, get a limo and look at art. Then sneak out of town. The art don't tell anybody I've been looking at it. It's just my little thing.

1078. Over here in the right margin, I am being encouraged to pick between Jason Statham and Vin Diesel. My God, what a challenge! Also, that's where famous artist go.

1079. I miss one thing: the days when I decided who was hip.

1080. If you need a quick Artist Statement just copy out 500 words of Hemingway, Celine, Ruskin or Barthelme. Impudence like this is hard to refute.

1081. I am in Santa Fe—neo Constable clouds, not much else.

1082. They were cold and ferocious, as I remember, and I was too and still am. Even so, except for Andy, they didn't suck up, and Andy made an art out of sucking up. Gee, not nice! What a downer. Look at that footprint on my face!

1083. Don Barhelme wrote well about "not knowing."

1084. Ban men. Suppress testosterone. Oh my. Nothing personal though, just my testosterone speaking.

1085. Excepting Don Judd (who was a lunatic), Bridget Riley, Peter Saul, and David Reed, artists don't write very good.

1086. I fell short of a synoptic survey.

1087. All of you know, in your hearts that "artist's statements" are bullshit. So why keep doing them? They are career-crippling documents. Many beholders think for themselves. Art is not evangelical testimony, I hope.

1088. If I live another 24 years, stuffing my pie-hole and filling out tax statements, I fully intend to sort out my thoughts. First question, what are thoughts, anyway?

1089. I would deal with "artists statements" as I dealt with the New Critics as an undergraduate. I would say, just fuck it and go live with the wolves. There's always time.

1090. Artist's statements are lies. We are rigorous. We don't fucking do lies.

1091. What if the artist is just flat wrong?

1092. Writing is hard, except the way I do it.

1093. Works of art start from numerous locations. Writing is always the same and, therefore, more competitive. You write one word. You write another word. You write another word—use colorful language when it is expedient. Greeting cards to Moby Dick, all the same.

1094. Woody Allen is a good place to avoid. I like Hoodie Allen.

1095. Oscar Wilde remarked that Wordsworth went into nature and found "sermons in the stones." I think we do that now.

1096. Well, sight is the key. I don't know about vision.

1097. I like Bridget on Nauman. I heard Peter Saul give a lecture on Picasso, just fuckin' great.

1098. I cannot tell you the level of contempt a professional writer feels for artist's statements.

1099. If critics were good painters they would be deeply compromised by that practice. Artist's statements are fig leaves. Without them artists would be free but also naked.

1100. I like Whitman and Rauschenberg as a pair, prolific sloppy fags, my boys! Democrats.

1101. Goya could really stick your face in the shit. I just don't think individual works of art can outstrip their audience and perform globally.

1102. There are dates on most art, in that any one who is vaguely familiar with the discourse can place most twentieth century art within 18 months of its making. There are so many tells. Even so, Van Gogh proliferates.

1103. Did Warhol create the base constituency for same sex marriage? One could argue that as Andy turns into history.

1104. Size, materials, horizon-line, haptic surface, color vocabulary all date works of art.

1105. Andy was not politically motivated. His work had enormous political consequences. Trace the progress of my late friend Lance Loud.

1106. My idea is that abstract expressionism is the bastard child of the muralistes. All those post offices in the west.

1107. What does it mean that an Ellsworth Kelly can move you, physically, around the room?

1108. Jasper and Bob didn't like Andy because he was so out-of the closet. Really flagrant in the early days. Nor did Johnny Myers, or any of the established gays in the art world, and there were a lot of them.

1109. DeKooning drawings kick some ass.

1110. Andy was flagrant but comfortable, like a dead spot in the room.

1111. Judd was a great artist whom I did not like because once the bounce of his reductive method wore off, it all looked like office furniture.

1112. I think it was my friend Jeremy who coined the phrase "Abstract Repressionism." As true as not true.

1113. Andy brought cool people, smart people and silly people together. I'm not crediting Andy. I just witnessed the consequences of his wickedness.

Andy had Catholic politics but he wanted to make the world safe for Andy who was very strange. There were other strange folk, like myself, who took encouragement from his sissy bravery.

1114. The word intention is not in my vocabulary.

1115. Andy was a director not an actor, maybe a model, but never actor. Actors are never in control.

1116. I was over at Vernon Fisher's studio back when he showed with Barbara Gladstone. While we're sitting there, Barbara called about one of Vernon's paintings: Barbara's question: "Hey Vernon, What's the rap on this thing?"

1117. If you didn't learn most of this stuff in school, you have been screwed.

1118. JGR is a prince. Has pissed off more people than I have.

1119. I am waiting for something new. I used to think the next big thing would be dust bunnies. Art is the consequence of saying the word.

1120. I'm a pretty alienated duck. Pushing who? Following who? I just dither along.

1121. I had a very nice dust bunny named Lazlo who lived under my couch in Ocean Beach.

1122. Difficulty is a prerequisite. If everybody likes it, I don't care about it. I am an adept.

1123. Where I grew up, one didn't adapt.

1124. What else were Stella's Protractors—serial work that closed the gate to failure and success.

1125. I regard intellectual discourse as a sky full of stars. If you work your whole life you can make maybe one or two of them twinkle a little brighter.

1126. The Protractors would cover an earthquake crack.

1127. I am out on the bright green lawn with two German Queens. Roy is holding a giant white tiger with blue eyes like baseballs on a choke chain that wouldn't restrain a cocker spaniel. Roy says, "Hey, pet the baby!" My manhood is on the line so I pet the tiger.

1128. Even if you don't win, you can die like a winner.

1129. Work is not labor. It's fun.

1130. I like falling sports. Surfing, Diving, Skiing, Riding. Anything where you lean forward and give yourself up.

1131. Gertrude Stein: There is no such thing as repetition. I repeat, there is no such thing as repetition. I think Gertrude means that the value accrues.

1132. Critique hovers somewhere between the hand and the eye.

1133. You must store your work with obsessive neatness.

1134. Picketty kind of marches along, not offensive, reader friendly, very old school—kinda Simon Schama for the leather jacket left.

1135. I was educated as an undergraduate by some very uppity new critics, and the difference between the new critics and the structuralists is that new critics were devoted to the text rather than the institution. Also, French Theory is more synoptic, more of a theory. New criticism is more atomic with major interpretations arising from an eccentric reading of a single trope.

1136. Let me be very clear on this. I am a critic not an apostle I teach every text I teach critically. No fuck-up or aporia goes unwinkled out. That is what critics do.

1137. French theory is bad because it has no heart. It is good because it has no soul.

1138. John Silber wasn't nice but he was quick with his little flapping wing. He would back you up to the fireplace and argue with you while slapping his withered arm on the mantle. Very disconcerting.

1139. There are no art critics anymore. Just "tastemakers."

1140. Art magazines wouldn't publish anything negative without printing something positive as a companion. Editors of art magazines completely capitulated to their advertising people. All downhill from there. Also, universities got really dumb—I mean really dumb.

1141. I don't have a job. I don't have any work. I am sick, sitting in bed, typing things in the desert. And I am not complaining.

1142. There are five corporate writing jobs in the art world. I am the sixth, and I am way too bad for suits.

1143. The distinction I have always made is that the dynamics of text are issues of force—the text forces up meaning. The dynamics of institutions are built around about power—the exercise of which manifests institution in the boarder culture. I am always interested in what's it good for.

1144. Not in family-friendly, slow-pitch America.

1145. I had Latin from high school. Mostly just wanting to read cool books and swan around like an elitist swine.

1146. I have friends who would call Derrida's iteration as "indexical." Maybe so.

1147. Pragmatism begins here: The meaning of a sign is the response to it.

1148. I think "Art in the Age of Mechanical Reproduction" is just flat wrong and romantic to boot.

1149. I don't believe a word of Lacan. Nor Freud. Predators both. Sigh-cology, as my friend Peter Saul would say.

1150. I am interested in art. I care nothing for the sigh-cology of the creator.

1151. Even Donald Fucking Kuspit agrees that it doesn't exist. Why would anyone care?

1152. Isaiah Berlin on Middle European Culture: There is nothing straight.

1153. Inanimate sigh-cology doesn't exist. Works of art are inanimate, or I really hope they are.

1154. I am a Foucaultian in that I would like to dehumanize everything and see what we might see.

1155. Art objects in the flow of time are animated by any number of contradictory atmospheres. I like to strip away the sociology, and address the object's propensity for endless rereading and misreadings.

1156. I would like to be Lewis Carroll interpreted by Deleuze.

1157. Peter Saul is precedent to Freud and not an emotional predator.

1158. About Saul and Freud: I meant morally precedent.

1159. Artists never improve their chances by putting themselves at an intellectual dis-advantage.

1160. My friend Christopher Knight said: The best thing about democracy is that anybody can be an elitist. Also, you can be a democratic elitist.

1161. Morning and evening. Work before and after. Not a big social life here in Fantasay. Also, I am a professional. I go fast. Quick and dirty to a high finish.

1162. I think the toxicity wears off a Bob's forty-year horizon. Not an event horizon. Rather the reverse.

1163. A rose is a rose is a rose is eros.

1164. The quality of the work is the quality of the execution. The quality of the job, is the quality of the endeavor.

1165. I like work as a vocation.

1166. Just considering the "history" I have lived through, the reportage seems a little shoddy and the prophecy a little self-serving.

1167. I put up the traffic signs. For what? We just jug on.

1168. I cannot bring myself to agree with that doofus Alan Watts.

1169. More weird than a faculty meeting.

1170. History is bullshit. I take the trajectory of Joan Mitchell's career as an example. She was mean. They didn't like her. She was a great painter who rescued painterly abstraction from expressionism.

1171. Bob's erasure reversed the sequence with which it was drawn. Way cool, I thought.

1172. Our job is not popularity. It is to make good art.

1173. The virtue of having a big present is that it keeps more pieces in play. Fewer pieces stuck in the road-tar of "history."

1174. My favorite ice-cream flavor is trout.

1175. Say it ain't so. I was quoted in a Guardian piece saying that I was writing a book called "Pagan America." One line yielded 2500 posts consigning me to hell. Mercy, Grace, Forgiveness, Redemption.

1176. As to Frankfurt school, I am not a fan of sociology.

1177. Benjamin and Adorno are snobs. No more lyric poetry when that's just what we need. Oh please. More butterflies swooping through the gravestones.

1178. There is just too much old-school German anti-enlightenment wooziness in Adorno and Benjamin. I hate feelings in criticism.

1179. I consider such criticism intellectual pornography, that little lovey bounce.

1180. Bataille? Good but good for what. Not criticism. Not fiction, just flogging the pony. And itsy bitsy whiffs of shame. Oh my!

1181. I read everything once. Adorno and Benjamin twice. I read biographies of both. All I got was big brown rooms, big fat furniture, and privilege. It is a totally alien world—as alien as Heidegger's university life. I used to teach Isaiah Berlin's "Three Critics of the Enlightenment" because it was written in English. It's my fault I'm sure, but I just can't get around the smug romantic Marxism. "Tis a failing I'm sure."

1182. Colin Rowe was a drunken child. I am just deferring my enthusiasm for fairy-tales.

1183. I don't want to talk about Germans anymore. I know it. I don't like it. I am a Mediterranean person. I did meet Adorno once, at Stockhausen's in Brentwood, across the street from O.J.'s. He had on a white jacket and a pink shirt. He did not respond to shallow American politesse.

1184. Charles Sanders Peirce, (purse) founder of pragmatism and the greatest logician of the century.

1185. I have thought about Adorno. I did not like the man, fine. I didn't particularly like Foucault who, in many ways, is my main dude. My problem with Adorno and Benjamin is that they dwell comfortably in a slightly faulty atmosphere of consciousness, and consciousness is not my métier. To be blunt, I never found anything in them that I could use in my profession, a lot of angst and inevitability, to be sure, but I dwell in the realm of mute objects. They dwell in social atmospheres. Just another world. No harm. No foul.

1186. Picasso: The hand knows things the eye cannot imagine

1187. Handmade Ben Day, like Gober does handmade ready-mades. I come from theoretical linguistics, chin deep in digital. The images are sleek, impenetrable, sex for the eye. Just not my kink.

1188. Fuck the hand. Fuck human. I want haptic, tactile, fractal. About one thousand times more information and ambient entropy.

1189. Two rules: Permission, Forgiveness; Permission, Forgiveness (repeat and fade).

1190. I have seen a lot of teacher-student jealousy. I always thought I was being forgiven for this by being a critic.

1191. The best teacher I ever had was Nathalie Sarraute, the French Novelist and Lawyer. One chilly diva. The worst teacher I ever had was Gordon Lish at Colombia, a twirling asshole, who ruined Raymond Carver's life, although Raymond helped. I just sat there stunned at the lies about Hemingway's method. I was but a child, at the time, but I could write.

1192. Artist with a Ph.D. is a travesty. Look that up.

1193. Oh. I should do mine! As a kid being dragged along La Cienega by my mom: A big hot hard-edged Fred Hammersley turned me on. As a young adult, December 1966 I walk into Ad Reinhardt's Black Show at the Jewish Museum. All day long I had been looking at abstract expressionist paintings that seemed to be shouting at me, and there was Ad black and exquisite, murmuring and very much alive. Stayed there for hours. Changed my life.

1194. No one as fond of thalo green and alizeran crimson even qualifies as an illustrator.

1195. Art education must presume an enthusiasm for art. Music is what we are.

1196. Words don't help art. They are words.

1197. Just because it's stupid, [it] doesn't make it art.

1198. Stupid won't disqualify you.

1199. What other artist other than Joan has changed so spectacularly for the better since her death! Joan's my peach. No expression. All anxiety.

1200. Riopelle was a fart.

1201. Artists don't grow. Works of art don't grow. They are manufactured, one by one, and sometimes they get better. Usually they just get bigger but they didn't grow that size.

1202. I'm sorry if you feel put upon, but you must remember the art you make is not yours. The culture owns a lion's share.

1203. Most of the great artists I know will tell you that making good art was a matter of decision. Andy was making homosexual-dc-dads, one day, the Superman. You either know your taste or you're a victim of it.

1204. Inner mind is not reliable. It makes excuses for our failures.

1205. We call this the "crises of technique" if you made them cry sincerely, can you just do its again and make them cry cold-bloodedly. The questions is, is this really just a technique?

1206. I am bi-technical.

1207. Decision is a step off into oblivion, over the lip of the wave.

1208. It's just a shot away. It's just a shot away.

1209. Good art give you more. It's a gift.

1210. Good trumps original.

1211. We never talk about good art because any inference of quality requires discrimination.

1212. I do miss teaching. I revel in the profound gaps of understanding. I am only shocked by the fact that the kids blow up at the mention of values. Good Art. Bad Art, Like that. Strange.

1213. I had a couple of Alberses for a while. They just did not hold up on the wall. My living room started looking like an abortionist's office in West Hollywood. I bought some time with them.

1214. Ferocity plays a key roll. Inspiration is for lotus-eaters. We regular practitioners got to play hurt.

1215. Rauschenberg: "I am never playing. I am working. Playing is for senior faculty members who are losing their faculties."

1216. Nothing about art is subjective, except the infelicities. Art is stuff, language, and objects. Embrace what you will, but chose with authority.

1217. Oh my, have you tried drinking your own urine?

1218. I keep telling you it's not sex: Vita Brevis, Ars Longa. Especially videos of running water, or the fog lifting, or Elka's blonde skeins flowing in the wind.

1219. Artists wear out techniques like babies wear out shoes, or should.

1220. I exempted Guston too. Really, I did. In my head, you know. I exempted Guston. My point: This is a slap shot, but all too sincere. I just hate provincial whimsy. Choo-choos and blue berry bushes.

1221. Pseudo primitive is better than pseudo intellectual? This would argue for the cult of sincerity. At my first gallery in Texas, we had a bumper sticker that said, "Sincerity is for Sissies!"

1222. Peter Saul is not faux anything, Maybe he's super-naif. I mean, oil glaze on DayGlo!

1223. Also, Peter writes words better than any visual artist I know.

1224. Cult of Persephone, in my reading, implies some agricultural fall and ascent. Maybe I should check. Farming and Arting are not the same, I hope.

1225. I prefer facture to creation. Nobody but my mom created anything cool, quoth Zarathurstra.

1226. De-skilling devolved from the idea that works of art are distinct from works of decorative art, in that works of art do not contain intrinsically valuable components like diamonds and gold. Marxists construed this distinction to encompass the invested skill of the artist: so "good" artists did not invest their skill. So politically acceptable art embodied no skill. I am not gung-ho on this construction, but all I have to do is think Fifties to like the Combines. You can't do that, of course.

1227. Buy Hartsfield. Dump Haacke and Buren. Hold Kelley.

1228. The issue with junk and *objet trouvé* is the same problem with photography. Do you want to look a something you've already seen marginally enhanced?

1229. Gober is very difficult to write about. You must judge the size of the wound by the size of the bandage.

1230. I am going to go look at my Ellsworth Kellys and Joel Shapiros and go to lunch.

1231. Boy do I hate glue-guns in the hands of idiots.

1232. Bob said history begins twenty years ago. I'd say ten today. Marxists sound like weenies trying make history today.

1233. I am all for the NEA in its support of cultural institutions like the symphony and the opera. This is heritage investment. Funding contemporary art is fucking with society. Umberto Eco said much the same when he declined the position of minister of culture in Italy.

1234. The government empowering fucking with society, is like mounting structuralist critique of institutions in an institution. It just doesn't happen. Never. Nobody feeds the mouth that bites without their pound of flesh.

1235. Don't fuck with Ad Reinhardt. First work of art I ever bought.

1236. Before the NEA and Nixon's tax maneuver, you could sell paintings to people with fluid incomes. They could give them to museums if the wheels came off. I would price it up, they would get their tax break. This is why there is so much late sixties and early seventies art in museums.

1237. Even when I was doing it, it looked like we were taking food from the mouths of children to finance upper middle class white kids who went to Yale. Did not feel good.

1238 Art does not exists in the service of public virtue, or shouldn't, because it's public.

1239 My experiences with alternate spaces in the heartland. You walk in. There is a guy in the back writing grants. There is a block of ice melting in a pan in the show room. No shipping, no insurance, no security. No good art except for treasures from the local junkyard. Bad wine. Plastic glasses. Little squares of cheese width toothpicks in them.

1240 American society is adversarial, not hierarchal. It values normality not excellence. Personally, I like Ruscha's painting: Mean as Hell. Just fucking live with it. 'Twas ever thus. No one cares. Art is not a required course. Thank God.

1241. I prefer my friends succeeding so I can hang in the guest house and nibble tiny quail.

1242. Works of art acquire interest by the complexity of their own internal sets of expectations and deferrals. Good things work on their own. They get better in context.

1243. I admit to being a bit of a catcher in the rye for young artists who come from rough circumstances and probably need it less. My bad.

1244. California and New York are no longer different, except they are.

1245. New York is structure. California is chemistry. Vegas is my stardust duvet.

1246. The young artists of yesterday would steal shit. The young artists of today are seminarians, like architecture students. They used to be different from one another.

1247. TED Talks are like the texts of Cheerios boxes. Except for the one on endosymbiosis.

1248. Wit, candor and manners will get you into a restaurant that closed years ago.

1249. I like Jacqueline Lichtenstein's "The Eloquence of Color," It's about the French Academy, but it is really a critique au clef of the contemporary art world.

1250. My position on social media unfriending: There are all these lobster tanks in Vegas. You always have to pick the one you kill. I know nothing about lobsters so I just stand there till one of those crustaceans really pisses me off!

1251. I'm beginning to have doubts about "culture" as an applicable category, and peoples too. Culture, it seems to me, is the most dispensable of critical categories, one of those things we notice burning on the highway. Do we prefer quiche, tacos, borscht, dim sum? Whatever we prefer today, we probably won't tomorrow. Culture in the German sense is dissolving. The definition I prefer is David Hume's suggestion that culture is what survives its maker and its patron. Peoples. What the hell are peoples? Some conservative brand of genetic segregation? Words survive their meanings.

1252   The state protects us with the constitution. It provides according to our deficit conditions—in 18th century that means wickedness. The state wants to keep things normal. Consumption balanced with production, until the last decade. In any case, fall behind or surge ahead and you will hear from them.

1253.   Half the art I see accuses me implicitly of being a sexist or a racist. I try not to be either. Makes me blue to bear the brunt of tenured purity.

1254.   I think we fight. Get off our asses and flight for justice. There are no rights that are not won. By this I mean that I do not hold with woozy ideas about "natural rights." I live toe to toe with "nature." We fight for justice, and we fight every day. Even on the Upper West Side.

1255.   Everybody hates an art critic, in my experience. I love the look that says, "You could help me but you won't!"

1256.   I think the trope that artists are sensitive is much overblown. Most of the great artists I have know are ferocious and would not be great artists if they weren't.

1257.   You have a right to your opinion, although this "art writer" writes better than any art critic in the last fifty years.

1258. Okay, we're in the cockpit of the Bellagio fountains with Steve Wynn and Bob Rauschenberg. Steve is showing off his new water dances. After about the fourth, Rauschenberg says: "Up? Why only up?"

1259. The culture is traversing swampy ground. We should try to civilize things as best we can.

1260. Artists do not produce children. They manufacture orphans.

1261. 98% of everything is shit.

1262. Whenever I read, or watch documentaries, about Andy Warhol the entourage around him looks sad and desperate. Yet I know you where there and speak of how fun and intellectually stimulating it was. So, what am I missing?

1263. I consider most of Andy's retinue to have been among the beguiled. Billy Name, Ultra Violet, Lou Reed, Sterling Morrison, and Henry G. were among the quick then and now the dead.

1264. And Andy, of course, who was less of a queen than he pretended to be.

1265. I co-produced and co-wrote on a documentary on Andy for PBS. Thanks to a director who fell in love with Andy, it was way too sentimental. I still got a Peabody and PBS got their Famous Gay American points.

1266. I feel fun on the horizon, and it scares me.

1267. The arrival of fun scares me because I have been predicting it for so long. Serious, secret, smarts fun.

1268. Everybody will talk about history. Nobody will talk about art.

1269. We must be enraged by history to make a difference.

1270. My advice is always conquer where you are. Then move outward.

1271. My position on relational aesthetics is that it generalizes itself into sociology. My position on this would be in line with Foucault's contempt for sociology. Grad school stuff.

1272. Two options. Buying on the way down erodes the flip-ability of a work. It might be art. Buying from the bankruptcy auction just starts the cycle again with a lower ante. Artists derive no benefit from all this kerfuffle.

1273. If you flip, you never know if the art will last. This is always an instance of *mauvaise foi.*

1274. About Too Big to Fail. If you're too big, you've already failed.

1275. This from Max Hutchinson, a dealer from the seventies: "Anybody who can't sell a handful of air with an idea in it, doesn't deserve to be an art dealer."

1276. I think art should just move next door.

1277. Technology is not science. Representations are not art. Technology and representations are prosthetics, as Derrida would have it.

1278. Not liking Marina Abramovic is a steady state condition, however, as an employee of the Guggenheim should know, Air kisses.

1279. Let me be clear. I don't "like" Abramovic's art, but she seems to be a lovely person, and the person ain't the art. The person is never the part. To think so is to indulge in rapacious faculty spite. So here's to you, Marina, wherever you art.

1280. I'm not saying Jeff is not a good artist, just not that good. The Henny Youngman of art.

1281. Jeff Koons is K2. If you're on that precipice, it's downhill in every direction.

1282. I'm working on it.

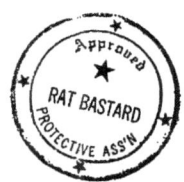

Approved
RAT BASTARD
PROTECTIVE ASS'N

‖P¢P‖